"COME AND YOU WILL SEE!"

"COME AND YOU WILL SEE!"
St. John's Course in Contemplation

PAUL HINNEBUSCH, O.P.

ALBA · HOUSE   NEW · YORK
SOCIETY OF ST. PAUL, 2187 VICTORY BLVD., STATEN ISLAND, NEW YORK 10314

Library of Congress Cataloging-in-Publication Data

Hinnebusch, Paul.
    Come and you will see! : St. John's course in contemplation / by Paul Hinnebusch.
        p.   cm.
    ISBN 0-8189-0580-8
    1. Bible. N.T. John — Meditations. 2. Contemplation.
3. Spiritual life — Catholic authors. I. Title.
BS2615.4.H55   1990
226.5'06—dc20   90-32186
                                                          CIP

Designed, printed and bound in the United States of America by the Fathers and Brothers of the Society of St. Paul, 2187 Victory Boulevard, Staten Island, New York 10314, as part of their communications apostolate.

© Copyright 1990 by the Society of St. Paul

Printing Information:

Current Printing - first digit 1 2 3 4 5 6 7 8 9 10 11 12

Year of Current Printing - first year shown
    1990   1991   1992   1993   1994   1995   1996   1997

Contents

Introduction vii
1. Come and You Will See 3
2. St. John's Course in Contemplation 9
3. The Witnesses Say, "Come and See!" 13
4. We See When Jesus Trusts Himself to Us 17
5. The Gentiles Come to See 21
6. They Shall Look Upon Him Whom They
   Have Pierced 27
7. Who Is This Son of Man? 35
8. I Am "I AM" 45
9. John 8:28, An Invitation to Salvation 51
10. "I AM" the Revealer 57
11. The One Who Tells Us Everything 61
12. "If You Knew ... Who Is Saying to You ..." 65
13. "Behold Your Mother!" 73
14. Responding to Mary's Presence 79
15. The Seven "I AM" Statements 85
16. "Whom Are You Looking For?" 89

Introduction

How This Book Came to Be

The theme of this book was originally developed by the author in a course he taught on St. John's Gospel in 1967. He developed the theme more fully in a course he taught in 1988. This time the students responded so well that the author decided to reproduce it in the present book form.

The inspiration for the theme of the book came from some pages in Marie-Emil Boismard, *Du Baptême à Cana* (Paris: du Cerf, 1956), pp. 74-77.

Credits

Chapters 1-4 were inspired chiefly by the above mentioned book by Père Boismard, O.P. Chapters 5-6 were inspired in part by Père Boismard's article,"La Royauté du Christ dans le quatrième évangile," *Lumière et Vie*, 57 (1962), pp. 43-63.

The development of chapter 7 was guided by an article by Yves-Bernard Tremel, O.P., entitled, "Le Fils de l'homme selon Saint Jean," *Lumière et Vie*, 62 (1963), pp. 65-92.

The chapters on "Jesus as 'I AM' " (8-10) were inspired

by Philip B. Harner, *The "I AM" of the Fourth Gospel* (Philadelphia: Fortress Press, 1970), and enlarged with the help of Raymond E. Brown's *The Gospel According to John* (Anchor Bible 29), pp. 536-537.

Chapter 12 was inspired by St. Thomas Aquinas' commentary on John 4.

The theological reflections in the chapters on "Behold Your Mother" (13-14) were inspired chiefly by the encyclical letter of Pope John Paul II, entitled, "The Mother of the Redeemer" (March 25, 1987). Quotations from this letter will be indicated by the symbol MR followed by the number of the paragraph from which the quotation is taken.

For much of the "fleshing out" of the various presentations, especially chapter 9, I am indebted to Rudolf Schnackenburg, *The Gospel According to St. John* (Vol. I, New York: Herder and Herder, 1968; Vol II & III, New York: Crossroad, 1987 & 1982). My interpretation of Nathaniel under the fig tree (chapters 3 and 4) is that of Schnackenburg.

In my classroom notes of 1967 and 1988, unfortunately I did not record my sources. Therefore, I cannot recall to whom I am indebted for some of the important ideas of this book, e.g., the basic idea developed in chapter 15.

Scriptural Quotations

Since nearly all the quotations in this book are from the Gospel According to John, whenever I quote from that Gospel, I give only the chapter and verse numbers, without "Jn."

Throughout this book we have used the New American Bible, with the revised New Testament, except where we have noted otherwise. Quotations from other translations are indicated by a letter after the chapter and verse indication, as follows:

- d - Douay-Rheims
- j - The Jerusalem Bible
- k - The New Testament, translated by Kleist and Lilly
- n - The New American Bible when the unrevised New Testament is used
- nj - The New Jerusalem Bible
- r - The Revised Standard Version

"COME AND YOU WILL SEE!"

1

Come and You Will See

"Come and you will see!" (1:39). This is the second sentence Jesus speaks in St. John's Gospel. He is answering a question two disciples have asked of him, "Rabbi, where are you staying?" (1:38). But their question in turn was in response to the first words Jesus speaks in John: "What are you looking for?" (1:38).

Because the two disciples accept the invitation to come and see, eventually they see Jesus where he dwells permanently in the Father's glory. And thus, too, they discover what they are really looking for in life. They find the answer to the most fundamental question that can be proposed to any human person, "What are you looking for in your basic life-search?" Jesus asks this question of all of us in his first words in John's Gospel.

Very often we find that when Jesus makes a statement in John's Gospel, the persons with whom he is speaking understand him at an immediate natural level. But he is really speaking at a higher spiritual level. Therefore, he speaks again, trying to lead his listeners to understand him at this higher level. At Jacob's well, for example, Jesus tells the Samaritan woman that if she would ask him, he would give her living water (4:10). She thinks he is speaking about ordinary, natural water: "Sir, you do not even have a bucket, and the cistern is deep" (4:11). But he is speaking of the spiritual water which leaps up to eternal life (4:14).

Or again, Jesus says to Nicodemus, "Amen, amen, I say to you, no one can see the kingdom of God without being born from above" (3:3). Nicodemus misunderstands. He thinks Jesus means that a person must be born again from his mother's womb (3:4). Jesus clarifies his statement, saying, "Amen, amen, I say to you, no one can enter the kingdom of God without being born of water and spirit" (3:5).

In the whole passage from John in which Jesus speaks his first words (1:35-39), the various statements are to be understood at two levels. One day John the Baptist was standing with two of his disciples, "Fixing his eyes on Jesus who was walking by, he said, 'Behold the Lamb of God' " (1:35, k). "The two disciples heard what he said and followed Jesus. Jesus turned and saw them following him and said, 'What are you looking for?' They said to him, 'Rabbi, . . . where are you staying?' He said to them, 'Come and you will see.' So they went and saw where he was staying, and they stayed with him that day. It was about four in the afternoon" (1:37-39).

When Jesus says, "What are you looking for?" the words are to be understood first at the immediate natural level. But we are meant to see also the spiritual meaning behind them. On the immediate level, the question could mean merely, "Is there something I can do for you?" But more profoundly, the question means, "What are you searching for in life?"

When the disciples reply, "Rabbi, where are you staying?" all they are looking for is a chance to talk to Jesus. They want an undisturbed conversation with him. They call him "Rabbi." Rabbis were interpreters of the Scriptures. The two probably wanted to ask him what the Scriptures say about the Messiah. "Rabbi, where are you staying?" simply means, "Where are you lodging? Can we come and have a private talk with you?"

If they are looking for a chance to speak with Jesus, it is because they are looking for something deeper. Whether they realize it or not, they are searching for the meaning of life.

"What are you looking for?" is the first question that Jesus puts to anyone who would like to follow him and be his disciple. The question really means, "What do you want out of life?" It concerns the basic need of every human person, a need which causes each of us to turn to God.

If the question, "What are you looking for?" is to be understood on this deeper level, so too the answer of the two disciples, "Where are you staying?" is to be interpreted at the same theological level. Whether he or she knows it or not, every human person wishes to stay with God.

The word "stay" (*menein*) is a key word throughout John's Gospel. It is variously translated as "stay," "abide," "dwell," "remain," "live." Repeatedly Jesus tells his disciples to remain in him, to abide in him, to live in him. And he tells them that he and the Father, in turn, will dwell in them (e.g., 14:23; 15:9).

When Jesus asks, "What are you looking for?" and the disciples answer, "Rabbi, where are you staying" they do not yet know clearly what they are searching for in life. That is why they want to speak with Jesus. In saying, "Where are you staying?" they do not realize that they are searching for where God dwells.

Jesus answers, "Come and you will see!" They come and stay with him the rest of the day, many hours, for it was only four in the afternoon when he said, "Come and you will see!" We are not told one word of their long conversation together. But whatever was said, it was only a beginning. For those words, "Come and you will see," also must be understood on a profound spiritual level. "Come and you will see" is an invitation to discipleship. Follow me, not just this afternoon to my lodgings. Follow me not just today or tomorrow or the next day. Follow me all the days of your life! Come with me and you will see where I dwell permanently, the place from which I have come, the place to which I will return.

The words, "Come and see," echo and reecho through John's Gospel. Eventually at the end of our Lord's life on earth, the night before he was crucified, the disciples get a deeper answer to their question, "Rabbi, where are you staying?" They will hear Jesus say, in his final prayer at the Last Supper, "Father, I want those you have given me to be with me where I am, so that they may always see my glory" (17:24, nj).

And where is Jesus? He is forever with the Father. He is "the only Son who is close to the Father's heart" (1:18, nj).

When the disciples, therefore, ask, "Rabbi, where are you staying?" the answer, "Come and you will see," is an invitation to follow him till at last they see him at home with the Father, and stay with him, not just from four o'clock till the end of a day, but for eternity: "Father, I want those you have given me to be with me where I am" (17:24).

But we must remain with him now if we would remain with him in glory. We must stay with him not simply by walking with him and talking with him. The disciples who came with him to see and remained with him throughout his days on earth eventually heard him say at the Last Supper, "Remain in me, live on in my love" (cf. 15:9). In a later response to their original question, "Where are you staying?" Jesus said to them on Palm Sunday, "Whoever serves me must follow me, and where I am, there also my servant will be" (12:26). And where is Jesus? He is lifted up on the cross. There too his servant will be, for only by way of the cross will his servant come to be with him where he is in the Father's glory.

On another occasion, those following Jesus heard him say, "Whoever eats my flesh and drinks my blood remains in me and I in him" (6:56). Jesus dwells in the believer and the believer dwells in him. Jesus is at home in the believer together with the Father, and the believer is at home with them: "If anyone loves me, he will keep my word, and my Father will love him, and we will come to him, and make our home with him" (14:23, r).

Whether they know it or not, then, in asking Jesus, "Where are you staying?" the two disciples are asking for the answer to the most basic question of human life, "What are you looking for?" We do not know exactly what we are looking for. So Jesus challenges us to follow him, saying, "Come and you will see."

When we see, we have the answer. We are seeking to find God and dwell with him, to stay with him forever with his only Son. And we dwell with Christ in God only because the Father and the Son are at home in us.

2

St. John's Course in Contemplation

The words of Jesus, "Come and you will see," are a challenge to believe in him. Throughout John's Gospel, believing is described as "coming" to Jesus and as "seeing" with divine perception.

> Whoever comes to me will never hunger,
> and whoever believes in me will never thirst (6:35).
>
> If anyone thirsts, let him come to me;
> let him drink, who believes in me (7:37, n).

These verses are Semitic synonymous parallelism. In such parallelism, a statement is made and then restated in other words. It is clear from these parallel statements that to come to Jesus is to believe in him.

Moreover, to believe in Jesus is to see him with faith's perception. "Everything that the Father gives me will come to me... For this is the will of my Father: that everyone who sees the Son and believes in him, may have eternal life" (6:37, 40).

In these words eternal life is promised to those who come to Jesus, see him with faith's perception, believe in him. Coming, seeing, believing, are three ways of saying the same thing. "Come and you will see" is Jesus' challenge to believe.

John the Baptist had already thrown down this challenge to look upon Jesus with perceptive faith: "Behold the Lamb of God!" (1:36). John himself sets the example. "Fixing his eyes on Jesus who was walking by, John said, 'Behold the Lamb of God!' " (1:36, k). That sentence is rendered poorly in most English translations. One version reads, "As he watched Jesus walking by." Even more weakly, another says, "And he looked towards him." In the original Greek, however, the evangelist said vigorously, "Fixing his eyes *intently* on Jesus as he walked by, John said, 'Behold the Lamb of God!' " (1:35).

He did not just take a quick look. He focused the full attention of his eyes and his heart upon Jesus. According to the Greek grammarian Zerwick, the Greek verb is an intensive form: "Fixing his eyes intently. . . ."

John the Baptist lovingly focused his attention upon Jesus and said, "Behold the Lamb of God!" "Behold him," that is, hold on to him by looking at him lovingly and attentively. Contemplate him! You are invited to see ever more wonderful things in him.

That was John the Baptist's invitation. Jesus repeated it in saying, "Come and you will see!" (1:39). Thus John 1:35-39, and indeed John's whole Gospel, is a little drama symbolizing everyone's life quest. Every life is a search, a seeking, a following, a finding, a remaining with God, a dwelling with him.

Even as the first chapter of John progresses, the disciples begin to see more deeply into Jesus. At first they see him only as Rabbi, a teacher (1:38). After being with him for a few hours, they see him as the Messiah, the Anointed One of God (1:41). They see him as the one about whom Moses wrote in the Law and also the prophets — that is, the great Prophet whom Moses said God would raise up after him (Dt 18:18). But they still see him as a man from Nazareth, the son of Joseph (1:45). They do not yet see him as the only Son of God.

Nathaniel sees him as one who looks right into one's heart. He acclaims him "Son of God and King of Israel!" (1:49). But this does not mean that he sees the divinity of Jesus. "Son of God" in the Old Testament was merely one of the titles of the king of Israel, whom God adopted as his son at his coronation (cf. Ps 2).

The chapter ends with Jesus saying, "You will see greater things than this.... Amen, amen, I say to you, you will see the sky opened and the angels of God ascending and descending on the Son of Man" (1:50-51). As we shall explain in a later chapter, the title of Jesus "Son of Man" tells us more about him than the title "the only Son of God" (1:14, 18, 34).

Such, then, is the challenge of Jesus at the beginning of John: "Come and you will see!" Your journey with me has just begun. You have barely begun to see. You will see greater things. Stay with me! Continue to look intently, contemplate lovingly, and you will come to see ever more clearly who I am, and what I am for you.

The word "Behold" (*ide*) occurs repeatedly in John's Gospel, and is very important (1:29, 36; 19:4, 5, 14; 19:26-27; 20:27 and 1:47; 11:36; 12:19). It is a clue to the nature of this Gospel. John's whole Gospel is an inclusion between two occurrences of the word "Behold" (1:23 and 20:27), thus indicating that the theme of this Gospel is beholding the Lamb of God.

John's Gospel is a contemplative look at Jesus, a profound contemplative interpretation of who Jesus is and what he is for us. It is an invitation to contemplate these realities again and again, and thus come with Jesus to where he is in the eternal Father's heart. It is also an invitation to contemplate and savor the presence of the divine Persons who dwell in our hearts even now (14:23).

To read John's Gospel rightly is to take a course in contemplation. John teaches us to focus our whole mind and heart eagerly, lovingly, longingly, attentively upon Jesus, and thus come to an ever more profound knowledge of who he is and what he is for us as Lamb of God. To see him is to see the Father (14:9). To come to him is to come to where he is, in the heart of God. "Did I not tell you that if you believe, you would see the glory of God?" (11:40). "Philip, whoever sees me, sees the Father" (14:9), now and in eternity.

The theme "Come and see" finds its final expression at the end of John when Jesus invites Thomas to *see* his wounds: "Put your finger here and behold (*ide*) my hands, and bring your hand here and put it into my side, and do not be unbelieving, but believe" (20:27). Thomas answered him and said, "My Lord and my God!"

Thomas sees not just wounds in the body of Jesus. With fully enlightened faith, he beholds his crucified and risen Lord and God. The seeing that is necessary, the seeing to which Jesus has patiently led his followers, is the beholding in faith. Only if we contemplate him in faith will we at length come to see the glory he had with the Father before the world was made (17:5, 24).

3

The Witnesses Say, "Come and See!"

It is not just Jesus who says, "Come and see." Those who have come and have seen in turn say to others, "Come and see!" The Samaritan woman left her water jar at the well and went into the town and said to the people, "Come and see a man who told me everything I have done!" (4:29) Those who have seen him become his witnesses to others. Philip told Nathaniel that he had found the Messiah. When Nathaniel doubted, Philip said, "Come and see!" This means, "Give him an honest hearing and see for yourself!"

It is not enough to be told about Jesus by a preacher or other witness. We must receive the Lord's intimate personal witness in our hearts. We must come into his presence and listen to him in Person. We must contemplate him directly, fixing the eyes of our hearts upon him. Such was the case of the first Samaritan believers. The woman's witness led them to Jesus. And by the power of his word, the Word in Person bore witness in their hearts. The evangelist writes:

> Many of the Samaritans of that town began to believe in him because of the word of the woman who testified, "He told me everything I have done." When they came to him, they invited him to stay with them; and he stayed there two days.

Many more began to believe in him because of his word, and they said to the woman, "We no longer believe because of your word. For we have heard for ourselves, and we know that this is truly the Savior of the world" (4:39-42).

There is no mention of signs and wonders worked in Samaria. Jesus' word was enough. The power of the word speaking in their hearts had won them over.

This faith of the Samaritans is a rebuke to those to whom Jesus had to say, "Unless you see signs and wonders you will not believe" (4:48). The Samaritans believed without signs and wonders, just like the first disciples who followed Jesus. We must give Jesus an honest hearing, and be moved by the power of his word, the interior word of grace, his intimate personal witness in our hearts. We must fix the eyes of our heart attentively upon him in love, and contemplate him in his word, and he will reveal himself to us, too. What do we see when we come to him with the Samaritans? Nathaniel saw him as King of Israel for, with Philip and Andrew and Peter, he had been looking for the Messiah of Israel. But the Samaritans saw him as Savior of the world. They were foreigners, despised by the Israelites. But when Jesus spoke to their hearts, they said to the woman, "We know that this is truly the Savior of the world" (4:42).

When we accept the invitation to come and see, and stay with Jesus as those first two disciples did, and fix the eyes of our hearts attentively upon him, he personally will open our hearts to his ever fuller self-revelation. It is not enough for us to look. He has to reveal himself interiorly in our hearts.

Jesus "stayed there two days" with the Samaritans (4:40). His ultimate desire is to stay permanently in our hearts, for he dwells in the hearts of those who love him and keep his word (14:23).

He is expert at opening our hearts to himself, as he

gently opened the heart of the Samaritan woman. He will reveal us to ourselves. He will show us our sinful hearts and thus reveal himself to *us* as *our* needed Savior.

He told the woman everything she had ever done. He showed her her need of a Savior so that she could lead the chorus of her townspeople in their proclamation of faith, "We know that this is truly the Savior of the world!" (4:42).

Thus we learn in John's Gospel not simply to behold the Lamb of God who takes away the sin of the world. We must see ourselves among those sinners whose sins he takes away. We learn to let him work personally in our hearts as he reveals us to ourselves as sinners.

Jesus sees into hearts. That is a characteristic of Jesus highlighted in John's Gospel. When Andrew brought his brother Simon to Jesus, "Jesus looked at him and said, 'You are Simon, the son of John; you will be called Kephas (which is translated Peter)' " (1:42). "Jesus looked at him." Jesus fixes his gaze lovingly and attentively upon our hearts.

This is even more striking in the case of Nathaniel. "Jesus saw Nathaniel coming toward him and said of him, 'Here is a true Israelite. There is no duplicity in him' " (1:47). Nathaniel said to him in reply, "How do you know me?" Jesus answered, "Before Philip called you, I saw you under the fig tree" (1:48).

What was Nathaniel doing under the fig tree? The fig tree was a symbol of messianic peace: "One nation shall not raise the sword against another, nor shall they train for war again. Every man shall sit under his own vine or under his own fig tree, undisturbed" (Mi 4:4).

In this peaceful situation, undisturbed by war and turmoil, a person would have the leisure to study the Scriptures and contemplate God. The Jewish rabbis had a phrase, "To sit under the fig tree," signifying a person's leisurely studying of the Torah.

Sitting under the fig tree, Nathaniel may well have been reflecting upon Psalm 32 to which Jesus alludes in saying, "Behold a true Israelite in whom there is no guile" (1:47, r). The psalm reads, "Happy is he whose fault is taken away, whose sin is covered. Happy the man to whom the Lord imputes no guilt, in whose spirit there is no guile" (Ps 32:1-2).

Reflecting on these words of the psalm, perhaps Nathaniel had just sincerely confessed his sins to God in his heart, and had received forgiveness. Jesus' knowledge of this deep secret of his heart amazes Nathaniel and he professes his faith, "Rabbi, you are the Son of God, you are the king of Israel" (1:49).

Thus by revealing Nathaniel's heart to him, Jesus reveals himself to Nathaniel. Nathaniel sees him as the Messiah. But he will progressively see ever greater things of Jesus, as Jesus progressively reveals himself ever more fully to those who have come to see and have remained with him.

4

We See When Jesus Trusts Himself To Us

We cannot come to a perfect seeing of Jesus unless Jesus entrusts himself to us. Seeing Jesus is not merely the fruit of our efforts in lovingly fixing our attention upon him. If we are to see, Jesus must manifest himself ever more fully to us, he must entrust himself to us. He entrusts himself, he reveals himself, only if we have the right quality of faith. Speaking of imperfect faith which is still too dependent upon the seeing of signs and wonders, the evangelist says:

> Many began to believe in his name when they saw the signs he was doing. But Jesus would not trust himself to them, because he knew them all, and did not need anyone to testify about human nature. He himself understood it well (2:23-25).

Jesus knows our hearts, and reveals himself fully only to hearts that are right. The fullest revelation comes when he entrusts himself to believers by coming to them and dwelling within them: "Anyone who loves me will be true to my word, and my Father will love him; we will come to him and make our dwelling place with him" (14:23, n).

If Jesus is to entrust himself ever more fully to us, if he is to reveal himself to us ever more clearly, we need certain qualities of heart. Some of these basic dispositions are revealed in Nathaniel: "Behold (*ide*) a true Israelite in whom there is no guile" (1:47, r). Behold Nathaniel, Jesus says, and you will see a quality of faith which you need if you, too, are to see greater things.

We must not only behold Jesus directly. We must also contemplate others in their relationship with Jesus to learn how to be open to his progressive self-revelation. Certain dispositions are necessary if we are to see Jesus as the Lamb of God who takes away our sins.

What dispositions do we see in Nathaniel? We see in him the characteristics described in Psalm 32, which Jesus alludes to in calling him a true Israelite without guile.

The person in this psalm is one whose sins have been taken away. They are taken away because that person has been candid, sincere, guileless in admitting and confessing his sin. He has not tried to cover his guilt or explain it away. He has not tried to deceive himself into thinking that he is not guilty. In short, there has been no duplicity in him.

These are necessary characteristics for recognizing and receiving Jesus as the Lamb of God who takes away the sin of the world. The sinner who explains away his guilt does not come to the Light. He does not want his sins to be exposed; he has hidden them even from himself (3:20). Frank simplicity and straightforwardness are necessary if we are to see Jesus ever more clearly.

Nathaniel had these characteristics. He wore no masks. He did not have one face for wearing in public and another for private use. He spoke spontaneously what was in his heart: "Can anything good come from Nazareth?" (1:46). In him there was no pretense. "Blessed are the pure of heart, for they shall see God" (Mt 5:8).

When Jesus calls him a true Israelite in whom there is no duplicity, he may well be contrasting him with Jacob, the one to whom God had given the name "Israel" (Gn 32:29). Jacob was a liar, a cheat, notorious for his duplicity (Gn 27:35-36). Hosea accuses the Israelites of his time of that same lying and cheating which had characterized Jacob, their ancestor (Ho 12:3-4).

The Book of Genesis loves to present popular etymologies, little folk-stories explaining how people got their names. In popular thinking, "Israel" means "One who sees." The people thought of Jacob as one who had seen God. He saw the ladder with angels ascending and descending upon it, and he saw God standing there beside him (Gn 28:13). Israelites, his descendants, were people who expected to see God. John's Gospel teaches us how to see God in Jesus. Jesus tells his disciples and Nathaniel that they would see the heavens opened and angels of God ascending and descending upon the Son of Man (1:51).

But like Jacob, their father, Israelites were very prone to duplicity (cf. Ho 12:3-4). Thus they were false to their call to see. Duplicity is a great obstacle to seeing God.

Nathaniel, a man in whom there is no duplicity, is a true Israelite, a model for all who want to see God. This contrast of Nathaniel with Jacob the liar at the beginning of John's Gospel, is a foreshadowing of the theme of blindness in John's Gospel, the theme of those who remain in the darkness of unbelief. It partly explains why so many of his contemporary Israelites rejected Jesus.

Their hearts were not sincere. They were not wholehearted towards God, but were self-seeking: "How can you believe," Jesus asked them, "when you accept praise from one another and do not seek the praise that comes from the only God?" (5:44).

Later Jesus levels an even worse accusation against

them. They are liars like their father, the devil: "You belong to your father, the devil.... When he tells a lie, he speaks in character, because he is a liar, and the father of lies" (8:44). Their duplicity prevents them from accepting Jesus when he speaks the truth (8:45).

Jesus cannot entrust himself to such as these. He reveals himself and gives himself as Savior, as Lamb of God sacrificed for our sins, to those who candidly, frankly, sincerely admit and confess their sinfulness. Once their sins are forgiven and they love him and keep his word, he entrusts himself fully to them: "Anyone who loves me will be true to my word, and my Father will love him; we will come to him and make our dwelling place with him" (14:23, n).

Nathaniel and the disciples who follow Jesus with hearts free of duplicity will see that Jesus is the true ladder of Jacob. What that ladder is will become clear when they contemplate the Son of Man lifted up: "You will see the sky opened and the angels of God ascending and descending on the Son of Man" (1:51).

Jesus not only reads hearts. He changes hearts. He changed the heart of the Samaritan woman. He changed the hearts of doubters into believers. Nathaniel had doubted that anything good could come out of Nazareth, but Jesus changed that into belief. He changed the heart of the doubting Thomas into the believing Thomas who saw Jesus in his glory and professed his faith in him: "My Lord and my God!" (20:28).

5

The Gentiles Come To See

The great crowd that had come to the Feast of Passover took palm branches and went out to meet Jesus as he entered Jerusalem. With deep frustration, the Pharisees said to one another, "Behold, the whole world has gone after him" (12:19). The evangelist wants you and me to behold this with delight. We are to behold the Savior of the World.

In saying, "The whole world has gone after him," the Pharisees were using hyperbole, meaning only that multitudes were following Jesus, and they were upset by this. But the evangelist, in reporting their statement, intends an ironic play on the words they spoke, "the whole world." He wants us to think of Jesus as universal Savior who will indeed draw all to himself.

As a sign of this drawing power, some Greeks want to see Jesus (12:20). Thus the "come and see" theme reaches a climax and a new beginning. The coming of these non-Israelites foreshadows how the Gentiles will come and see Jesus in the full light of faith when he is lifted up and draws all to himself (12:32).

Leading up to the coming of these Greeks, the evangelist had referred five times to God's intention to save the Gentiles through Jesus. Now, like the first fruits of the nations, these Greeks come and want to see Jesus.

The evangelist's first reference to universal salvation is the declaration of the Samaritans, "We know that this is truly the Savior of the world" (4:42).

The next reference comes when Jesus speaks of the other sheep, not of the fold of Israel, whom he must bring into the one fold by laying down his life for the sheep (10:16).

The third reference comes when Caiaphas unwittingly prophesies universal salvation: "He did not say this on his own, but since he was high priest that year, he prophesied that Jesus was going to die for the nation. And not only for the nation, but also to gather into one the dispersed children of God" (11:51-52).

The fourth reference is in the acclamation of the crowds as Jesus enters Jerusalem riding an ass. In their acclamation, the crowds quote from Zechariah's prophecy of a king who will bring peace to all nations:

> Fear no more, O daughter Zion,
> Behold your king comes,
>   seated upon an ass's colt (12:15; cf. Zc 9:9).

By alluding to these words of Zechariah, "Behold your king comes," the evangelist is preparing us to behold the King of the nations lifted up and reigning from the cross. The coming of the Greeks asking to see Jesus is the sign that these prophecies of universal salvation are about to be fulfilled.

We are not told whether Jesus actually met with this little group of Greeks. But his immediate response to their request to see him is his discourse beginning with the words, "The hour has come for the Son of Man to be glorified" (12:23), and ending with the words, "And when I am lifted up from the earth, I will draw all people to myself" (12:32).

The Gentiles Come To See

He will be glorified by the coming of the nations to him when he is lifted up on the cross in his hour.

Thus the coming of these Greeks to see Jesus has a symbolic meaning. The evangelist presents it as an interpretation of the crucifixion as a power drawing all people to Christ. The coming of the Greeks and the discourse it provokes is like a guide to the contemplation of the Lord's passion. It gives an advance explanation of its meaning and power. It is as if the evangelist were saying, "Behold, this is what you are to see as you contemplate the passion of Jesus."

The passion story in John's Gospel begins with the quotation from Zechariah, "Behold your king comes" (12:15), and ends with another quotation from Zechariah, "They shall look upon him whom they have pierced" (19:37). In everything framed between these two quotations, we are to contemplate the crucified King: "Behold your king" (19:14). Jesus reigns from the cross. His crucifixion is his exaltation, his glorification. Jesus explains all this when the Greeks come asking to see him.

He takes their coming as a sign that his hour has come, "Andrew and Philip went and told Jesus. Jesus answered them, 'The hour has come for the Son of Man to be glorified'" (12:22-23). Jesus has just been formally rejected by the plot of the leaders to put him to death. Caiaphas had said, "It is expedient that one man die for the people" (11:50). But in his death, God's plan "to gather into one the children of God who were scattered abroad" (11:52) will be fulfilled. The hour has come for this to happen. "The hour has come for the Son of Man to be glorified."

His rejection by his own people and their putting him to death results in the salvation of the nations. He will be glorified on the cross by drawing the nations to himself.

The desire of the little group of Greeks to see him symbolizes the desire of all the nations to see him. To all the nations, not just to those first two disciples, Jesus says, "Come and see!" All the nations are engaged in that same search expressed in the first words of Jesus in John's Gospel, "What are you looking for?"

This desire of the nations to see Jesus will be fulfilled when they look upon him whom they have pierced, that is, when they understand in faith the meaning of his crucifixion. The nations will be able to come to him and see him in the fullness of faith only as the fruit of his sacrifice, his lifting up.

If the nations are drawn to Jesus when he is lifted up, that means they come to him. But to come to Jesus is to believe in him (6:35; 7:37), and this is only because the Father draws them (6:44-47). The evangelist had begun this whole section by saying, quoting Zechariah, "Behold your king comes" (12:15). Jesus will reign as king when he is lifted up on the cross and when, with the fullness of faith and contemplative love, they look on him whom they have pierced. He will reign in the hearts of all who believe in him. And it is precisely his "lifting up," his sacrifice, his supreme revelation of God's love, which will call forth the faith of the nations. The Father will draw them to Jesus by the gift of the Holy Spirit, sent as the fruit of this sacrifice in which he is glorified (7:39).

Thus the "lifting up" of Jesus is his royal enthronement, because it draws forth faith from the hearts of people everywhere, and by that faith, the nations are subject to his reign.

The response of Jesus to the Greeks' request to see him means, "Come and see me lifted up. Contemplate me in my hour in which, by your response of faith, I am glorified in your hearts."

Thus again in this incident, "to see" is one of those enigmatic words which has to be understood on two levels.

The Gentiles Come To See

When the Greeks came to Philip and asked him, "Sir, we would like to see Jesus," the word "see" meant only, "We want to meet him." But in his response to their request, Jesus gives the word to "see" a spiritual meaning. To "see" spiritually means to believe everything about him which is discovered by those who "behold" him in contemplative faith. For example, it is to see him as Son of God: "For this is the will of my Father, that everyone who *sees* the Son and believes in him may have eternal life" (6:40). It is to see him as God's envoy, the one sent by the Father to reveal the Father: "Whoever believes in me believes not only in me but also in the one who sent me, and whoever sees me sees the one who sent me" (12:44-45).

Above all, it is to see him as the "I AM" lifted up for the salvation of all (8:24, 28).

Thanks to his "lifting up," the nations will come to believe in him. Thus it is of great significance that when Jesus is elevated on the cross, a pagan, a Roman soldier, pierces his side with a lance (19:34). John at once gave this a spiritual meaning, a fulfillment of Zechariah, "They shall look upon him whom they have pierced" (19:37; Zc 12:10). The pagans shall behold him and believe, whereas many in Israel will be blind (9:39).

When the unbelievers among the Jews reject Jesus before Pilate, saying, "We will have no king but Caesar," Jesus is lifted up, enthroned on the cross as King of the nations whom he draws to himself. Thus his crucifixion is truly his glorification, his lifting up is his exaltation. The nations, symbolized by the pagan soldier who thrust the spear into his side, "look" in faith "upon him whom they have pierced."

6

They Shall Look Upon Him Whom They Have Pierced

Now since it was preparation day, in order that the bodies might not remain on the cross on the Sabbath, for the Sabbath day of that week was a solemn one, the Jews asked Pilate that their legs be broken and they be taken down. So the soldiers came and broke the legs of the first and then of the other one who was crucified with Jesus. But when they came to Jesus and saw that he was already dead, they did not break his legs, but one soldier thrust his lance into his side, and immediately blood and water flowed out.... For this happened so that the scripture passage might be fulfilled... "They will look upon him whom they have pierced" (19:31-37).

It looked like those among the Jews who were responsible for our Lord's crucifixion were very zealous for the glory of God. They did not want the holy Sabbath to be desecrated by the presence of crucified bodies on the holy day. But perhaps there was a deeper motive for their haste in wanting the body of Jesus removed. When Jesus was lifted up, "Pilate wrote a title and put it on the cross; it read 'Jesus of Nazareth, the King of the Jews'... It was written in Hebrew, in Latin, and in Greek," so that people of all nations would be able to read it, for Greek and Latin were widely used throughout the Roman Empire. Thus Pilate displayed Jesus before "the whole world" as King of the Jews. Certainly, in keeping with Jesus' words, "When I am lifted up from the earth, I will draw everyone to myself" (12:32), the evangelist sees the crucifixion as the enthronement of Jesus as King of all nations. Those who were responsible for the death of Jesus were upset by Pilate's inscription. They pressed Pilate to get the execution over with as soon as possible. They asked Pilate that the legs of the crucified men be broken so that their bodies might be taken away. It was like saying, "Get Jesus out of sight as soon as possible. We don't want him to be displayed before the whole world as King of the Jews!" Out of sight, out of mind.

But God directs things differently. Through the instrumentality which these unbelievers used to get rid of Jesus, the whole world now looks upon Jesus as their King, "This happened so that the Scriptures might be fulfilled... 'They shall look upon him whom they have pierced' " (19:36-37).

What is the meaning of looking on the one who has been pierced? Does John mean they shall see Jesus in the parousia, when he comes as final judge of the world? That is how two other New Testament writers use the passage from Zechariah quoted here (Rv 1:7; Mt 24:30). But not so John. John means that believers, here and now, look on the pierced Jesus with loving contemplative faith.

The passage from Zechariah reads:

> I will pour out on the house of David and on the inhabitants of Jerusalem a spirit of grace and petition; and they shall look on him whom they have

thrust through, and they shall mourn for him as one mourns for an only son, and they shall grieve over him as one grieves over a first-born (Zc 12:10).

The Book of Revelation (1:7) combines the text from Zechariah with Daniel (7:13) thus showing that the one who comes on the clouds of heaven as Lord and Judge of all the world is the one who was crucified: "Behold he is coming with the clouds and every eye will see him, everyone who pierced him; and all the tribes of the earth will wail on account of him. Even so! Amen!" (Rv 1:7, r).

This verse from Revelation is speaking of the final coming of Jesus. The ones who pierced him in crucifixion see him as their judge. But their realization of who it is that they have pierced comes too late. Their wail of lamentation is over the condemnation the Judge will pronounce upon them.

Matthew, too (24:30), uses the text from Zechariah in combination with Daniel 7:13. He also refers to the final coming of Jesus: "Then will appear the sign of the Son of Man in heaven, and then all the tribes of the earth will mourn (Zc 12:10), and they will see (ibid.) the Son of Man coming on the clouds of heaven with great power and majesty" (Mt 24:30, r).

But when John in his Gospel says, "They shall look upon him whom they have pierced," he is not referring to the final coming of Jesus as judge. He is thinking more in terms of grace and salvation poured out here and now upon those who look upon the pierced one with loving faith and mourn for him in love and repentance. As witness of the blood and water coming forth from the pierced side of Jesus, he is appealing for this faith and repentance. John's use of the passage is more in keeping with the spirit of the original passage as it occurs in Zechariah.

In Zechariah, the passage deals with a great lament of Israel over a man who was killed. The people were not without guilt in this man's murder. Their lament is an expression of conversion, and brings the inhabitants of Jerusalem to a state of blessedness. God pours out a spirit of compassion and supplication over them: "I will pour out . . . a spirit of grace and petition, and they shall look on him whom they have thrust through" (Zc 12:10).

John quotes this passage just after telling how the soldier thrust a lance into Jesus' side and blood and water flowed out. No doubt he wants us to think of the fuller context of the passage from Zechariah which continues:"On that day there shall be open to the house of David and to the inhabitants of Jerusalem a fountain to purify from sin and uncleanness" (13:1).

Thus, in John's Gospel, to look upon the pierced one is to come to the source of forgiveness and grace, life and salvation.

We verify this interpretation of John 19:37 by fitting it into the theme of "looking" and "seeing" which runs throughout John's Gospel: "Behold the Lamb of God! Behold the man! Behold your king!" "Behold" is a formula of revelation. In John, it usually introduces a great truth which is to be contemplated in loving faith. "Behold," that is, "Look intently, fix the eyes of your faith upon this. Penetrate beneath the surface which immediately meets the eye. Gaze with contemplative love."

Each time the evangelist tells us to behold, he presents a further clarification of John the Baptist's words, "Behold the Lamb of God who takes away the sin of the world." He presents another aspect of the revelation contained in that statement.

John's Gospel is like a series of transparencies flashed on a screen before our eyes. I once attended a lecture on a great painting by Fra Angelico. Using transparencies, the lecturer called our attention to one aspect of the painting after another. His first transparency showed a very sketchy outline of the painting, simply showing the overall composition of the work, the striking juxtaposition of the various figures. Over this he laid another transparency which focused our attention upon certain other features of the painting. He laid one transparency after another over the ones he had already put down, each one showing us different elements which must be seen if we were to grasp the beauty of the whole. When the final transparency was laid down, we had the completed work before our eyes, so that in one glance we could appreciate the masterpiece before us, seeing simultaneously the marvelous harmony of its parts.

St. John's Gospel is like a series of transparencies, one laid over the other so that a glorious picture of Jesus is presented to our contemplative gaze. In the present transparency we are told to look upon him whom we have pierced.

This passage is just one of a series of transparencies in which we behold the Lamb of God. And we see the full richness of meaning in this particular passage focusing on the pierced side of Jesus only because we see it laid over a whole series of transparencies already presented to us. Each one of these enriches the meaning of the ones which the evangelist has already shown us. No passage in John is complete without the others.

In the first transparency, John the Baptist sees Jesus walking by. Fixing his eyes and heart intently upon him, he says, "Behold the Lamb of God!" Look intently upon this man, Jesus of Nazareth, and see him as the Lamb of God.

But thus far we see only the preliminary sketch, the general outline of the portrait. The features of the Lamb of God will be filled in by successive transparencies. All the other transparencies must be laid over this first one before we can see in full clarity what it means that this man, from the despised town of Nazareth, is the Lamb of God.

The evangelist lays down another transparency. "Just as Moses lifted up the serpent in the desert, so must the Son of Man be lifted up, so that whoever believes in him may have eternal life" (3:14-15).

This is the first of a series of Son of Man transparencies. In three of these, we contemplate the Son of Man as lifted up.

Moses told the people in the desert to look upon the bronze serpent he had lifted up on a pole. And all who looked upon it with faith were cured of the serpent bites. But how are we to look upon Jesus when he is lifted up on the cross? We, too, are to see him with the eyes of faith. "So must the Son of Man be lifted up so that everyone who believes may have eternal life in him" (3:14-15). Bodily eyes see a man nailed to a cross. The eyes of faith behold the source of eternal life.

Successive transparencies fill in the portrait of Jesus in ever greater detail. We will behold the Lamb of God in the way John the Baptist wants us to see him only when we have seen all the transparencies. For example, we must see the various ones presenting him as Son of Man, as lifted up, as pouring out from his pierced side the living waters of grace which take away sin and give eternal life.

In John's Gospel, the pierced side of Jesus is a symbol of the exalted Jesus, Jesus glorified by his life-giving power, which is signified by the blood and water gushing from his side.

Finally, looking with Thomas in the fullness of faith at the pierced side of the glorified Jesus, we contemplate as it were in one glance all that we have seen in all the preceding transparencies.

The heart of Jesus as venerated in the liturgy of the Solemnity of the Sacred Heart is a symbol of all that we behold as we contemplate Jesus lifted up and pierced with a lance and look upon those glorious wounds along with Thomas. We see not just the life-giving river flowing from his pierced side, not just the life-giving Holy Spirit symbolized by these waters. Above all, we see the love behind it all. "For God so loved the world that he gave his only Son, so that everyone who believes in him might not perish but might have eternal life" (3:16).

7

Who Is This Son Of Man?

When Jesus says that the Son of Man must be lifted up, the people ask, "Who is this Son of Man?" (12:34). To find the full answer to this question, we need to come and see Jesus in each of the passages in John's Gospel in which he is called "Son of Man." The portrait of Jesus, Lamb of God and Son of Man, is complete for us only when we have seen all the transparencies of which we spoke in the preceding chapter.

Jesus challenges the man born blind to whom he has given sight, "Do you believe in the Son of Man?" (9:35). In presenting this question, some of the ancient manuscripts of John substitute "Son of God" for "Son of Man." Evidently the copyist who changed John's original words thought that "Son of God" is a richer title than "Son of Man." But it is not. "Son of Man" tells us more about Jesus than "Son of God." This will become evident in the course of this chapter.

Jesus is called "Son of Man" thirteen times in John's Gospel, in nine different contexts. Do all thirteen texts present a unified, harmonious picture of Jesus, the Lamb of God?

Come and See the Ascending and Descending Son of Man

The first mention of the Son of Man in John's Gospel is a prophetic announcement. "Amen, amen, I say to you, you will see the sky opened and the angels of God ascending and descending on the Son of Man" (1:51). The last mention is the solemn affirmation of the fulfillment of this promise: "Now is the Son of Man glorified, and God is glorified in him" (13:31).

In between these two passages, the Son of Man is presented as making a journey. He has come down from heaven and is returning to heaven. The evangelist refers to this descending and ascending of the Son of Man in three different passages.

First, Jesus announces to Nicodemus that the Son of Man who came from heaven must return to heaven: "No one has gone up to heaven except the one who has come down from heaven, the Son of Man" (3:13).

Secondly, after the multiplication of the loaves, Jesus proclaims that he is the true bread come down from heaven who will return there where he was before: "I am the living bread that came down from heaven; whoever eats this bread will live forever" (6:51; cf. 6:33, 53). When many of his disciples who were listening were shocked at this and could not believe, Jesus says, "What if you were to see the Son of Man ascending to where he was before?" (6:62).

This means that in the Eucharist we eat the flesh and drink the blood of the risen and ascended Lord, the one who was lifted up and glorified. In the Eucharistic Lord, we need to see everything that John tells us about the Son of Man. He is the bread of God come down from heaven who, by being lifted up, has returned to where he was before. It is this glorified Son of Man who gives life in the Eucharist. It is his glorified flesh and blood that we eat and drink in the Eucharist.

The evangelist speaks a third time about the ascending Jesus when the risen Lord says to Mary Magdalene: "Stop holding on to me, for I have not yet ascended to the Father.

But go to my brothers and tell them, 'I am ascending to my Father and your Father, to my God and your God' " (20:17-18). The journey of the Son of Man is completed. The Son now draws to the Father all the children of God who had been scattered abroad. His journey empowers him to give life with God — eternal life.

The Lifting Up of the Son of Man

Another thread is woven into the theme of the journey. This is the theme of the lifting up and glorification of the Son of Man. The theme of the lifting up tells us more explicitly the nature of his ascending to where he came from. Three times Jesus refers to the lifting up of the Son of Man.

First, to Nicodemus, to whom he had just said, "No one has ascended to heaven except the one who descended from heaven, the Son of Man" (3:13). Jesus continues, "Just as Moses lifted up the serpent in the desert, so must the Son of Man be lifted up, so that everyone who believes in him may have eternal life" (3:14-15).

The one who has descended from heaven is the one who is lifted up on the cross. He ascends to the Father by way of the cross. The one who has been lifted up is the one who gives eternal life, because he has been lifted up.

Secondly, in the eighth chapter, to those who are stubbornly resisting believing in him, Jesus says that they will know who he is when they have lifted him up: "When you lift up the Son of Man, then you will realize that I AM, and that I do nothing on my own, but say only what the Father taught me" (8:28).

Thirdly, at the end of his public ministry, when the blinding of the unbelievers has been completed, Jesus again speaks of the Son of Man being lifted up. When the Greeks ask to see Jesus, he says, "The hour has come for the Son of Man to be glorified.... When I am lifted up from the earth, I will draw everyone to myself" (12:23, 32). The Son of Man is glorified in being lifted up. His full glory is revealed by the life-giving power of his death, his power to draw everyone to himself. The lifted up Son of Man gives life to the nations.

The three announcements of the lifting up of the Son of Man have been made. All that remains now is the accomplishment of the Son of Man's glorification when he is actually lifted up in his hour. This is the hour when Judas sinks into darkness and the Son of Man is lifted up into glory: "He took the morsel and left at once. And it was night. When he had left, Jesus said, 'Now is the Son of Man glorified, and God is glorified in him'" (13:30-31).

The Son of Man and Judgment

We must also consider briefly two other references in John to the Son of Man. Both of these are in the context of judgment. In John 5:27, the "Son" has the power to sit in judgment precisely because he is "the Son of Man," the one who descended from heaven and has ascended again by way of the cross: "For just as the Father has life in himself, so also he gave his Son the possession of life in himself, and he gave him power to exercise judgment, because he is the Son of Man" (5:26-27).

So too in a context of judgment, Jesus asks the man who had been born blind, "Do you believe in the Son of Man?" (9:35). When the man replies, "I do believe, Lord," Jesus says, "I came into the world for judgment, so that those who do not see might see, and those who do see might become blind" (9:39).

Do these two references to the Son of Man fall into the unity and harmony of the theme of the Son of Man as we have seen it so far, or do they strike a discordant note? How does the theme of judgment fit in with the picture of the Bread of Life come down from heaven for the life of the world and ascending to where he was before in glory from whence he bestows eternal life?

A coin has two sides. The opposite side of the Son of Man's life-giving power is his power of judgment. In the Old Testament, a judge always had the power over life and death. He could condemn a person to death, but could also judge that he should be allowed to live. Indeed, a judge's primary function was to safeguard life. These two functions belong to the Son of Man, and life-giving is the primary one: "Just as the Father has life in himself, so also he gave to his Son the possession of life in himself, and he gave him power to exercise judgment because he is the Son of Man" (5:26-27).

"Because he is the Son of Man," that is, he has power on earth to exercise judgment precisely because of everything which is expressed in the concept of Son of Man as presented by John, e.g., because he has come from heaven and has been "lifted up" to give life to the world.

The two sides of the coin, the power to give life and to pass judgment, were already introduced in the conversation with Nicodemus: "God so loved the world that he gave his only Son, so that everyone who believes in him might not perish but might have eternal life. For God did not send his Son into the world to condemn the world, but that the world might be saved through him. Whoever believes in him will not be condemned, but whoever does not believe has already been condemned because he has not believed in the name of the only Son of God" (3:16-18).

It is as the one lifted up that he gives life, and as the one lifted up he is the condemnation of unbelievers. Condemnation of those who do not believe is only a byproduct of his giving of life to those who do believe.

We shall discuss later whether Jesus is speaking explicitly of condemnation in saying, "When you lift up the Son of Man, then you will realize that I AM" (8:28). Is the emphasis here on condemnation, or, even here, is Jesus emphasizing his giving of life?

Angels of God Ascending and Descending

The picture of the angels of God ascending and descending on Jacob's ladder (Gn 28:12) provides Jesus with a striking symbol to show that he, the Son of Man, is the true way, the real ladder to God. He is the way to the Father only because he is the Son of Man descended from heaven and ascended again to where he was before: "Amen, amen, I say to you, you will see the sky opened and the angels of God ascending and descending on the Son of Man" (1:51). Later Jesus will say, "I am the way and the truth and the life. No one comes to the Father except through me" (14:16) — me in my sacrifice, me in my lifting up. All this is implied in the title "Son of Man." All this, Nathaniel, you will see in seeing the "greater things" (1:50).

Born From Above

The descending and ascending theme reveals what the Son of Man is for us. If he had not descended from God in the incarnation and ascended to God in the lifting up, no one of us would be able to go to God (3:13). Jesus makes this clear to Nicodemus.

When Nicodemus came to Jesus by night, he must have asked the question which preoccupied the Jewish teachers of his day: What is necessary for salvation? A rich young man had asked the same of Jesus, "What must I do to attain eternal life?" (Mk 10:17). A doctor of the law had also asked it, "What is the first of all the commandments?" (Mk 12:28). These questions are a closer focusing on the question: "What are you looking for?" which Jesus posed to the first two disciples (1:38). The rich young man and the doctor of the law were seeking eternal life, and have the notion that keeping the commandments is the way to it.

Whether Nicodemus explicitly asked this question or not, Jesus answers it. He tells Nicodemus that salvation is not primarily a matter of human effort, of the accomplishment of the law, but of being "born from above." "Amen, amen, I say to you, no one can see the kingdom of God without being born from above" (3:3). It is not a matter of what a person does, but of God's action upon that person. The new birth "from above" is an event which originates in heaven and is brought about by divine power beyond human control. It is the work of the Spirit who blows where he wills and over whom we have no control (3:8).

The words "born from above" have often been translated "born again," but "born from above" is the only justifiable translation. Perhaps the translation "born again" was influenced by Nicodemus' complete misunderstanding of what Jesus had to say. Nicodemus is the one who thought Jesus was saying that one must be born again, born a second time from his mother's womb: "How can a person once grown old be born again? Surely he cannot reenter his mother's womb and be born again, can he?" (3:3). Only Nicodemus, not Jesus, uses the word "*deuteron*," (a second time, again).

This sort of thing happens repeatedly in John's Gospel.

The hearers reach wrong conclusions because they fail to listen properly to what Jesus says. Jesus is then forced to speak again and explain the divine reality of which he is speaking, for his listeners have heard him on too human a level.

Therefore, Jesus says to Nicodemus who has misunderstood, "Amen, amen, I say to you, no one can enter the kingdom of God without being born of water and the Spirit" (3:5). That is what it means to be "born from above" (3:3).

In baptism, we are born from above of water and Spirit, not by any human effort and power, but sheerly by the power of the Holy Spirit who blows where he wills (3:8).

Thus the expression "born again," used only by the misunderstanding Nicodemus, should be avoided. Rather, we should use the expressions used by Jesus, "born from above" (3:3) and "born of water and Spirit" (3:5). The gift of life from above, eternal life, is given to us because we believe in the Son of Man who is lifted up (3:15), and express this belief by receiving the Spirit through baptism in water (3:5).

"No one has gone up to heaven except the one who has come down from heaven, the Son of Man" (3:13). Only because the One who descended from heaven has ascended to heaven by being lifted up can we be born from above, and so ascend into heaven with him.

Summary

As we follow Jesus through John's Gospel, we come to see ever more clearly who he is and what he is for us. The title "Son of Man" tells us more about him than his title "Son of God." "Son of God" tells us who he is, but of itself it does not tell us what he is for us, what he has done and is doing for us, and how he has done and is doing all this by his being lifted up and ascending to where he was before.

The thirteen texts in John which speak of the Son of Man form a consistent and well-knit whole. They tell us not only who Jesus is, but what he is for us. He has come down from heaven and has ascended again to where he came from. His return to the Father from whom he came is by way of his lifting up and glorification on the cross. He could be lifted up, crucified, only because, in coming from heaven, he became man. He is glorified in his lifting up, for thus as man he receives power over all flesh to give eternal life to all whom the Father gives him (17:2).

Thus this lifting up, this ascension to where he was before, is the source of eternal life which he gives as the living bread from heaven. In his lifting up, he takes away the sin of the world and bestows eternal life. When he is lifted up, he is recognized as "I AM," the one who bears the divine name, the one in whom God is present and active for the salvation of the world (8:28). (The meaning of the Son of Man as "I AM" will become clearer in the following chapters.)

Those who refuse to believe all that is implied in his name "I AM" die in their sins (8:24). They do not come to divine life. They remain under the condemnation which they have brought upon themselves. All judgment is centered in his person because he is the Son of Man, the giver of life as Lamb of God. One judges himself by his attitude towards the Son of Man.

Thus in the thirteen references to the Son of Man in John's Gospel, the evangelist does indeed present a unified and harmonious picture of Jesus as Savior of the world.

8

I Am "I AM"

The Son of Man calls himself "I AM." "When you lift up the Son of Man, you will realize that I AM" (8:28). We do not really know who the Son of Man is until we know that his name is "I AM," which is the name of Yahweh, the God of Israel.

"I AM" is the translation of John's Greek, *EGO EIMI*. Each time that Jesus says, "I AM," *EGO EIMI*, he is speaking in the same manner in which Yahweh speaks in Second Isaiah (Is 40-55). In those passages in which Yahweh says, "I am," or, "It is I," or, "I am he," the prophet is clearly stressing that Yahweh is the only God, and therefore he alone can save.

One of these passages, Isaiah 45:18, is of special significance in helping us to understand what Jesus means when he says, "I AM." The Hebrew reads, "I am Yahweh, and there is no other." The Greek of the same reads, "I AM (*EGO EIMI*), and there is no other." Thus the scholars who translated the Hebrew into Greek before the time of Christ interpreted "*EGO EIMI*, I AM," as the equivalent of "Yahweh." I AM is God's proper name.

When God revealed his name "Yahweh" to Moses, he said, "This is what you shall tell the Israelites: I AM sent me to you" (Ex 3:14). In the Greek Septuagint, this is rendered, "*EGO EIMI* sent me to you."

Second Isaiah is like a series of meditations on the name "Yahweh," and is filled with plays upon that name. The Hebrew of Isaiah 45:18 was one of those plays on that name: "I am Yahweh [i.e., I AM 'I AM'], and there is no other." The Greek renders this simply as, "I AM, and there is no other." Thus, in the Greek, *EGO EIMI* (I AM) is the proper name of God, who is the only God and Savior. In John 8:28, Jesus uses this name in referring to himself: "You will realize that I AM."

However, there was one shortcoming in the Greek translation, *EGO EIMI*. Later readers who came from a Greek culture tended to see this as expressing not God's unicity or oneness, but his existence. Yahweh, however, was not saying to Moses, "I am the Existing One," or, "I am Self-Existing Being." His existence was taken for granted. He is indeed self-existing, but to Moses he was speaking of something else about himself. He was stressing his active presence with his people. He was saying, "I am with you to save." That is how God revealed himself to Israel and how they experienced him. He was ever present with them, saving them. Yahweh really means, "I am with you to save."

In Second Isaiah, Yahweh is repeatedly asserting to his people in Babylonian exile the truth expressed in his name. He is comforting them by assuring them of his saving presence. It was as if he were saying, "Don't you know that 'I am with you' is my very name?"

Thus in Isaiah 45:18, "I am Yahweh, and there is no other" (Hebrew), "I AM, and there is no other" (Greek), the stress is not on God as the Existing One, but as the One present with his people as their only Savior. He alone can save because he is the only God, and he is assuring them that he is with them to save.

This is clear from the whole context of the passage:

> I am Yahweh, and there is no other,
>> I have not spoken from hiding
>> nor from some dark place of the earth,
> And I have not said to the descendants of Jacob,
>> "Look for me in an empty waste"
>>> (Is 45:18-19)

That is, I am right there with you where you are.

> Was it not I, Yahweh,
>> besides whom there is no other God?
> There is no just and saving God but me,
> Turn to me and be safe,
>> all you ends of the earth,
>> for I am God, and there is no other!....
> Only in the Lord are just deeds and power!
>>> (Is 45:21-24)

Thus when Jesus says of himself "*EGO EIMI* (I AM)," he is claiming that in him the one only God is present with his people to save them. In his own person, Jesus is the revelation and presence of the saving God, who alone can save. Nowhere but in Jesus can salvation be found.

This helps us to understand the Son of Man passage in John 8:28 where Jesus says, "When you lift up the Son of Man, then you will realize that I AM." You will realize that God is present in me to save you.

This is the second of the three passages in which Jesus speaks of the Son of Man being lifted up. In the first "lifted up" passage (3:14-15), we learn that the Son of Man lifted up is life-giving for those who believe, but is condemnation for those who refuse to believe (3:18). Which side of the coin — eternal life or condemnation — is emphasized in John 8:28, where Jesus is speaking explicitly to those who are resisting belief in him?

> He said to them again, "I am going away and you will look for me, but you will die in your sins. . . . For if you do not believe that I AM, you will die in your sins. . . . When you lift up the Son of Man, then you will realize that I AM, and that I do nothing on my own. . . . The one who sent me is with me . . ." (8:21, 24, 28, 29).

"When you have lifted up the Son of Man" (i.e., when you have crucified him) "then you will realize that I AM" (8:28). How should this announcement of Jesus be understood? In terms of damnation, or in terms of salvation? Is Jesus saying, "When you have lifted me up it will be too late, and you will know me only as the Judge who condemns you," or is Jesus saying, "When you have lifted me up, then you will come to the believing knowledge which will save you"?

At first sight the passage seems to be speaking of the condemnation of these people who are resisting faith in him. "He said to them, 'I go away, and you will seek me, and die in your sin; where I am going you cannot come'" (8:21). They will look for him, but it will be too late! They will remain under the universal condemnation of all sinful mankind. They will die in their sin, and so will not be able to go where Jesus is going as he ascends to where he came from.

They cannot go where he is going, for the reason Jesus had given to Nicodemus: "No one can ascend into heaven but the one who has descended from heaven, the Son of Man" (3:13). Jesus says to these people who are resisting faith in him, "You are from below, I am from above; you are of this world, I am not of this world" (8:23, r). Here, "this world" means those who resist God. They are alienated from him and hostile to him.

Jesus is not of this world. He is from above, for he has

descended from heaven and so he can return there. Their only way to go there is by believing in the one who has descended and ascended again, and thus, by being born from above, they will be empowered to go above. For, with Jesus, they will then be "from above," born from above of water and the Holy Spirit (3:3, 5).

But since they are resisting faith in him, Jesus adds, "That is why I told you that you will die in your sins. For if you do not believe that I AM [the One present to save you], you will die in your sins" (8:24).

By resisting faith, they are in the process of delivering themselves up completely and finally to the realm of death. But Jesus shows them the way to salvation. They must fight their way to the belief that Jesus is who he claims to be. He sums up this claim in an "I AM." "If you do not believe that I AM, you will die in your sins" (8:24).

In the other two passages where Jesus speaks of his lifting up, the verb is in the passive voice: "So must the Son of Man be lifted up" (3:14), and "Once I am lifted up, I will draw all people to myself" (12:32). God's decree requires that he be lifted up. This is God's plan of salvation.

But here in 8:28, the active form of the verb is used: "When you lift up the Son of Man, then you will realize that I AM." In other words, the unbelievers are held responsible. The handing over of Jesus is their fault. As Jesus later said to Pilate, "The one who handed me over to you has the greater sin" (19:11).

Therefore when Jesus says to them, "When you lift up the Son of Man, you will know that I AM," the implication seems to be that their sin will be clear to them, and their punishment a horrifying certainty.

But we must not be quick to jump to the conclusion that Jesus is already pronouncing their condemnation, or even that he is predicting it. Of course, if they do persist to the end in unbelief, they will be condemned. But there are various indications that salvation is the main idea in 8:28. And salvation is being offered to those who lift him up in crucifixion. This will be clearer in what follows.

9

John 8:28
An Invitation To Salvation

The background for John 8:24 and 8:28 in Second Isaiah helps us to see that these two sentences are not a prediction of certain condemnation, but are an invitation to salvation. The sentence, "If you do not believe that I AM, you will die in your sins" (8:24) is simultaneously a warning against unbelief and an invitation to believe. The other sentence, "When you lift up the Son of Man, then you will realize that I AM" (8:28) is thus an offer of salvation.

This interpretation seems to be verified if we look closely at the relationship between these two verses and two verses in Second Isaiah, namely, Isaiah 43:25 and 51:12.

In the Revised Standard Version, Isaiah 43:25 reads: "I, I am He, who blots out your transgressions for my own sake." In the New American Bible we find: "I, it is I, who wipe away for my own sake, your offenses." "I, it is I," and "I, I am He," are two different English translations of Isaiah's Hebrew *anoki, anoki hu*. The Greek Septuagint translates *anoki, anoki hu* as *EGO EIMI EGO EIMI*. That is, "I am 'I AM' who blots out your transgressions for my own sake." Thus the Greek makes the second "*EGO EIMI* (I AM)" a proper name of God.

The same thing happens in the Greek Septuagint for Isaiah 51:12: "I, I am he, that comforts you" (r); "I, it is I, who comfort you" (n). But the Greek reads, "I am 'I AM' who comfort you." The second "I AM" is God's proper name. The exiles were tempted to seek comfort in the Babylonian gods. Yahweh insists that he alone is their Savior, and he is with them to save.

When, therefore, Jesus refers to himself in John 8:24 and 8:28 as "I AM," he would have us realize that when he is lifted up in death and resurrection, he is the I AM who blots out sins and comforts his people.

Therefore, we can paraphrase John 8:24 and 8:28, saying, "When you lift up the Son of Man and come to realize that I AM, you will be comforted if you believe that I AM, for I will blot out your transgression for my own sake, even your sin of killing me."

But if you persist in unbelief and refuse to "come to believe that I AM, you will surely die in your sins" (8:24).

Also in Isaiah 43:25, our background for John 8:24, 28, God is telling his resisting and rebelling people that he will forgive their sins and comfort them, not because they deserve it, but for his name's sake: "You burdened me with your sins, and wearied me with your crimes. Yet I am 'I AM' who wipe away for my own sake your offenses, your sins I remember no more" (Is 43:24).

"I AM" God Present to Save

Another text from Second Isaiah is also apropos here. God is carrying on a lawsuit with the nations. He calls the Israelites as witnesses "to know and believe in me and understand that it is I (*ani hu/ EGO EIMI*). . . . It is I, I the Lord; there is no savior but me" (43:10-11). That is, I am "I am

An Invitation to Salvation

with you." I am the only one who can save you. The Israelites are to believe and experience this truth, and witness to it before all the nations. "You are my witnesses, says Yahweh. I am God, yes, from eternity I am He (*EGO EIMI*)" (43:12).

So too in John's Gospel, Jesus is involved in a lawsuit with "the world." He himself is the one on trial. Who is guilty, Jesus or the world? "Can any one of you convict me of sin?" (8:46). When the Spirit comes, the Paraclete, he will testify on behalf of Jesus, and convict the world of sin (16:8-9).

Thus, the point of the words, *EGO EIMI*, I AM, on the lips of Jesus is this: God is present in Jesus and speaking in him, declaring that he is the eschatological savior. God is acting in Jesus saving the world. He is not just the savior of Israel from exile in Babylon, as in Second Isaiah, but he is the savior of the world.

We are now ready to look at the entire verse (Jn 8:28): "When you lift up the Son of Man, then you will realize that I AM, and that I do nothing on my own," that is, God is acting in Jesus, "but I say only what the Father taught me" that is, God is speaking his saving word in Jesus. Jesus is the sacrament of God's saving presence and power in the world.

To sum up, Jesus is using the name I AM in exactly the same way Yahweh uses it in Second Isaiah. In saying I AM, Jesus is saying much more than that he is God. He is saying that He is God-present-to-save. He is affirming that God is present and acting in him: "You will realize that I AM and that I do nothing on my own, but I say only what the Father taught me. The one who sent me is with me . . ." (8:28-29).

So it is not just a matter of recognizing his divinity when he is lifted up, but a recognition of God's presence and action in him saving the world.

It is precisely as lifted up on the cross that I AM saves the world. It is this we must recognize, this we must believe.

The crucified I AM is God saving the world, saving us, the very people who lifted him up in crucifixion. "The one who sent me is with me" even on the cross, working your salvation in me. "He has not left me alone, because I do always what is pleasing to him" (8:29). I do only his work; he does his work through me. "I and the Father are one" (10:30). "Realize that the Father is in me and I am in the Father" (10:28).

There are other examples in John showing that Jesus, in applying to himself the name "I AM," is revealing God's presence to save. Indeed, he is the sacrament of that presence. He is the revelation and the reality of God's saving presence. This thought is expressed in a variety of ways in John.

Thus, in his final prayer at the Last Supper, Jesus sums up his ministry as making known the Father's name to his disciples, that is, as revealing the very reality of God. "I revealed your name to those whom you gave me out of the world" (17:6). This means, I am the manifestation of your presence in power to save, for in Semitic thinking, the name is the person who bears the name. "Whoever has seen me has seen the Father" (14:9); that is, whoever sees me sees the Father's saving presence. This seeing, of course, is the seeing in faith.

Indeed, Jesus says that the Father has given him his own name. "Keep them in your name which you have given me. When I was with them, I protected them in your name that you gave me" (17:11-12).

This means that God has given Jesus not just his divinity, but also his own presence in power to save and protect. That is why he consecrated Jesus with divinity — to send him to save (cf. 10:36).

Furthermore, "the hour" that brings the glorification of Jesus brings the glorification of the Father's name. It will be

An Invitation to Salvation

manifest in "the hour" that God is present to save in the One who is lifted up: "The hour has come for the Son of Man to be glorified.... Father, glorify your name!" (12:23-28).

"Glorify your name" means the same as "Hallowed be your name" (Mt 6:9), which means, "May your saving work be accomplished!" (We shall say more about this in a later chapter.)

"Who, then, is the Son of Man?" (cf. 12:34). He is the man who calls himself "I AM, *EGO EIMI*," God present in power to save. Thus the title "Son of Man" says more about him than "Son of God," for it tells us not only who he is in himself as God, but what he is for us, God present in power to save us. Though he is Son of God, as man he can be lifted up on a cross to die, and as man be lifted up to the glory which was his before the world began (17:5).

Pilate brought him before the crowds wearing a crown of thorns and covered with the blood of the scourging. And he said, "Behold the man!" (19:5). When we behold the Man, hungry and thirsty and exhausted at Jacob's well, and crowned with thorns and nailed to a cross, we see the one whose name is I AM. "When you lift up the Son of Man, then you will realize that I AM" (8:28).

We have been beholding the Lamb of God. We have accepted his invitation to come and see. We have not seen all that we must see in the Son of Man lifted up till we have seen that we present-day citizens of Texas and Missouri, Australia and Norway, have lifted up the Son of Man by our own personal sins.

We must hear the lifted up Son of Man saying to each of us personally from the cross, "I am 'I AM' who blot out your transgressions for the sake of my name!" (Is 43:25).

10

"I AM" The Revealer

"I am," and "It is I," so often translated in the Greek as *EGO EIMI*, was an Old Testament revelation formula when spoken by God. Yahweh uses it repeatedly, especially in Second Isaiah, to reveal his saving presence. It is like saying, "Look, here I am! I am with you to save you." Ever since the days of Moses and the Book of Exodus, the name Yahweh has carried the overtones, "I am with you."

Jesus is using the same revelation formula whenever he says in John's Gospel *EGO EIMI* (I AM). He is exercising his function as revealer.

He says to the woman at the well, "I am He (*EGO EIMI*), the one who is speaking with you" (4:26). These words seem to be patterned on words of Yahweh spoken to the exiles in Babylon: "My people shall know my name. They will know when the day comes that it is I (*EGO EIMI*) saying, 'Here I am'" (Is 52:6).

Isaiah's second sentence is in parallel with the first: it restates the first sentence in other words. Clearly, God's name which shall be known is *EGO EIMI* (It is I), and he is speaking of his presence to save: "Here I am."

The prophet is meditating on the meaning of Yahweh's name, applying that meaning to the present situation, and finding comfort in it for the exiled people. The exiles in

Babylon are tempted to think that Yahweh has totally abandoned them, and are tempted to turn for help to the Babylonian gods. It is as if the prophet were saying to them, "Don't you know from your past history that 'Yahweh' means 'I am with you to save'? It means 'Here I am.' Your ancestors knew from the experience of his saving presence that Yahweh lives true to his name."

The prophet is assuring them that they, too, shall experience this saving presence: "My people will know my name" (52:6). The Hebrew word "know" expresses what is known by experience. They shall experience his saving presence when he brings them home from exile. "My people will know my name. They will know when that day comes that *EGO EIMI* is saying, 'Here I am.' "

These words are echoed in the words of Jesus to the woman at the well: "*EGO EIMI*, the one who is speaking with you" (4:26). The second phrase, "the one who is speaking with you," is in apposition to "*EGO EIMI*." This echoes Isaiah's words, "*EGO EIMI* is saying, 'Here I am' " (Is 52:6).

"My people will know my name." In the person of Jesus, they will experience Yahweh's saving presence. Jesus, who calls himself "I AM," is the revelation of God's saving presence.

As so often in John's Gospel, Jesus' words to the woman are to be understood on two or more levels. On the immediate level, which the woman understands, Jesus is simply saying, "I who am speaking to you am the Messiah." He is responding to her words, "I know that the Messiah is coming, the one called the Anointed; when he comes he will tell us everything." He says to her, "I am he (*EGO EIMI*), the one who is speaking to you." I am the One who tells you everything. I am the revealer of all truth.

But the evangelist expects us, his readers, to understand the words of Jesus at a deeper level. He wants us to hear Jesus saying, "The one whose name is 'I AM' is the one who is speaking to you." He is Yahweh present with you to "tell you everything." He is the revealing Word. For in his Prologue, the evangelist has already introduced Jesus to us as the Word. Therefore in this conversation with the woman at the well, we are to hear Jesus saying that he is not only the revealer, the one who tells us everything, but he himself is the Word, the fullness of divine revelation. Only in the Word can the inner life of God be known: "No one has ever seen God; the Only Son, God, who is at the Father's side, has revealed him" (1:18).

Truly, the words of Isaiah are fully verified in Jesus, God present with us to reveal and to save: "They will know when the day comes that IT IS I, saying 'Here I am' " (Is 52:6).

God reveals himself in Jesus, and speaks and acts in him so exclusively, that his salvation is visible and available only in Jesus. Because Jesus is perfectly God's Word, the Old Testament revelation formula, "I am he (*EGO EIMI*)" is rightly on his lips, since in this formula God reveals his presence as Savior.

* * * * *

The Latin Vulgate translation of John 8:25 is highly intriguing in the light of the explanation we have just given of John 4:26, "I am he, the one who is speaking with you." The Vulgate of 8:25 is *"Ego principium qui et loquar vobis,"* which translated into English is "I am the beginning, who also speak to you" (cf. 8:25, d). Jesus said this in answer to the unbelievers' question, "Who are you?"

The Greek text of 8:25 is very difficult to interpret. One would like to think that St. Jerome's translation in the Vulgate is correct, "I am the beginning, who also speak to you."

But contemporary scholars propose a variety of likely interpretations, e.g., "What I told you from the beginning."

The formula *EGO EIMI* on the lips of Jesus is no mere claim of equality with God, though his divinity is implied in such statements. Jesus is saying more: God is present in me to reveal himself, and there is no way to salvation apart from me.

Though *EGO EIMI* on the lips of Jesus stresses God's saving presence and power in Jesus, the full personal divinity of Jesus is also implied. When Jesus says, "Amen, amen, I say to you, before Abraham came to be, I AM" (8:58), the unbelievers tried to stone him for blasphemy (8:59; 10:33).

The great sin is to refuse to believe in the name of God's only Son (3:18), a refusal to believe in God's saving presence and power in Jesus, a refusal to believe in all that is implied in his use of the words, "I AM (*EGO EIMI*)." "For if you do not believe that I AM, you will die in your sins" (8:24). "Whoever does not believe has already been condemned, because he has not believed in the name of the only Son of God" (3:18).

Thus the name *EGO EIMI*, God's name, is glorified in the hour of Jesus' death and resurrection. In accepting his death as the fulfillment of his mission (12:27), Jesus says, "Father, glorify your name!" (12:28). The Father is glorified when Jesus is lifted up to draw all nations to God. The Father is glorified; that is, he is manifested as present in Jesus in power to save the nations. We, too, pray for this coming of all peoples to Jesus when we say, "Our Father . . . hallowed be your name!"

11

The One Who Tells Us Everything

We have seen Jesus at Jacob's well presenting himself to the Samaritan woman as the Revealer, the one who tells us everything.

The woman had brought up a controversial subject: Which is the right place to worship God, Jerusalem or Samaria? (4:20). Jesus gave her the answer, but she was not sure of his authority as a teacher, so she brushes his response aside, saying, "When the Messiah comes, he will tell us everything" (4:25). Jesus said, "I *am* he, the one who is speaking with you" (4:26). Thus Jesus claims that he is the One who tells us everything. He is the revealer of all truth. He has the answers to all of life's questions.

The Letter to the Hebrews says, "In times past, God spoke in partial and various ways to our ancestors through the prophets; in these last days he spoke to us through a son . . . who is the refulgence of his glory, the very imprint of his being" (Heb 1:1-3).

Because Jesus is the Son of God, the perfect image of the Father, he is the full and perfect revelation of God. Therefore John calls him "the Word." He is the Word which tells us everything. As the Word of God, he is both revealer and the fullness of the truth revealed.

What does he reveal? Above all, he reveals God the

Father. "No one has ever seen God. The only Son, God, who is at the Father's side, has revealed him" (1:18).

But in the very act of revealing God to us, the Word made flesh reveals us to ourselves. This is a very important point expressed by the Second Vatican Council:

> Only in the mystery of the Incarnate Word does the mystery of man take on light. . . . He who is "the image of the invisible God" is himself the perfect man. . . . By the revelation of the mystery of the Father and his love, Christ fully reveals man to himself, and makes his supreme calling clear (*Gaudium et Spes*, 22).

Only by grasping the truth revealed by Christ, the Word of God, do we really come to know who we are.

How does the Word tell us about ourselves? By his relationship with God. Because he is the perfect man, he reveals what every man or woman's relationship with God ought to be. John's Prologue tells us about the Word's relationship with God.

> In the beginning was the Word,
> And the Word was with God,
> and the Word was God.
> He was in the beginning with God (1:1-2).

The line, "the Word was with God," has been accurately translated, "the Word was in God's presence." This is because the Greek preposition "with" used here ("the Word was *with* God") implies motion towards. The Word was ever turned towards God. He was ever impelled towards God in love. He was totally focused upon God. The Word was in God's presence, fully aware of him in knowledge and in love. He was in perfect loving communion with God.

When the Word became flesh, he continued in the same relationship with God. He remained *with* God, ever turned towards him in love. He said, "Truly, truly, I say to you, the Son does nothing of his own accord, but only what he sees the Father doing" (5:19, r). "My teaching is not mine, but his who sent me" (7:16, r). "I speak of what I have seen with my Father" (8:38, r). "He who sent me is with me" (8:29, r). Whatever the Word reveals to us, he receives from God. He lives always in God's presence.

As the perfect man, Jesus reveals to us what every man and woman is meant to be. Every human person is called, like this Man, the Word, to be in God's presence, to be with God, turned towards him in knowledge and love, to live in loving communion with him, always receiving life and light from him.

All of this has been made possible for us by the Word made flesh. He said to us at the Last Supper, "If anyone loves me, he will keep my word, and my Father will love him, and we will come to him, and make our home with him" (14:23, r).

God wants to be at home in our hearts, at home in our love. A person is at home wherever he or she is lovingly welcomed. God wants to be at home in our welcoming love for him, and he wants us to be at home in his welcoming love for us. "If anyone loves me, he will keep my word, and my Father will love him, and we will come to him, and make our home with him" (14:23, r).

We see then what Vatican II means in saying that the Word made flesh reveals man to man. Man or woman is fully man or woman only when he or she is fully at home in God's love, and God is at home in that human person's love.

Such is the fullness of revelation brought to us by the Word-made-flesh, the revealer, the one who tells us everything, the one who by revealing God to us reveals us to ourselves, reveals that like himself we are to live forever in God's presence, completely turned towards him in the fullness of knowledge and love, always at home with the Father in a deep and loving communion.

The Word, the only Son of God, became man and lived among us, so that all men and women might always be at home in the loving presence of God.

We come to see all this when we accept the Baptist's invitation, "Behold the Lamb of God," and Jesus' invitation, "Come and you will see."

12

"If You Knew ... Who Is Saying To You"

> If you knew the gift of God and who is saying to you, "Give me a drink," you would have asked him and he would have given you living water (4:10).

"Living water" is one of those expressions in John that must be understood on two levels. On the natural level, living water simply means "running water." A great deal of the water used in the Holy Land is rain water gathered into cisterns. The pool of water in a cistern is not running water. But the water springing forth from a fountain or spring is. The stream of running water is inseparable from its source, and can be called "living" because it bubbles forth incessantly.

This imagery is found in Jeremiah where God calls himself the source of living water: "They have forsaken me, the source of living waters; they have dug for themselves cisterns, broken cisterns, that hold no water" (Jr 2:13).

The supernatural water which Jesus gives is called "living" because it is inseparable from its source. This "water" is life, divine life, and that is a deeper reason why it is called "living." Life is a persistent theme in John. Jesus is always talking about this life, and usually calls it "eternal life." In

John, the two terms "life" and "eternal life," as given to believers, always mean God's life as given to them.

The divine life Jesus gives is inseparable from its source. It dies in us if we are cut off from God, "the source of living waters" (Jr 2:13). The human life of a person is cut off from the life of the mother at birth, and the person thereafter lives an independent life. But not so with the divine life Jesus gives us. It cannot be lived cut off from Jesus who is its source. "Without me you can do nothing" (15:5). We must remain forever united with him. As a branch cannot live unless it remains in the vine, so we cannot live God's life unless we remain in Jesus, the true Vine (15:1-8).

But more specifically, what is this gift of God, this living water which Jesus gives? Is it the Holy Spirit? Is it the word of God? The word "gift" occurs repeatedly in John's Gospel, in different contexts. Sometimes the Son of God himself is the gift. "God so loved the world that he gave his only Son" (3:16). But in this Son, through faith in his name, we have the gift of eternal life, God's life in us.

In another place also the gift is Jesus himself. "It is my Father who gives you the real heavenly bread. . . . I myself am the bread of life" (6:32, 35, n). Later Jesus says, "The bread that I will give is my flesh for the life of the world" (6:51). This flesh given on the cross in sacrifice for us is Christ's gift to us in the Eucharist. But again, in that gift of himself we are given eternal life, God's life in us.

When Jesus says, "If you knew the gift of God and who is saying to you, 'Give me a drink,' " is the gift to which he is referring the Holy Spirit? In a later chapter, the Holy Spirit is called "living waters" (7:39):

> "Let anyone who thirsts come to me and drink. Whoever believes in me, as Scripture says, 'Rivers of living water will flow from within him.' " He

said this in reference to the Spirit that those who came to believe in him were to receive (7:37-39).

It would seem then that when Jesus says, "If you knew the gift of God," he is referring to the Holy Spirit. The living waters flow from within the believer because the very source of the waters of divine life, namely, the Holy Spirit, is within the believer.

Each of these passages speaking of a gift from God presents a different aspect of the one same reality, God's divine life within us, God's own life that we are living, God's life which we are incessantly receiving from him, "the source of living waters." The waters within us are living because they are not cut off from their living source, and that source is within us. "Whoever believes in me . . . , 'Rivers of living water will flow from within him' " (7:39). God's life is in us because God lives in us.

All this is the gift of God, and Jesus is the Giver. "If you knew the gift of God and who is saying to you, 'Give me a drink,' you would have asked him, and he would have given you living water" (4:10).

Jesus is presented in John's Gospel, both at the beginning and at the end, as the One who gives the Holy Spirit. John the Baptist testified to this: "The one who sent me to baptize with water told me, 'On whomever you see the Spirit come down and remain, he is the one who will baptize with the Holy Spirit' " (1:33). While gathered with his disciples at the Last Supper, Jesus promises to send this Holy Spirit. On the day of his resurrection, he fulfills this promise. He breathes on his disciples and says, "Receive the Holy Spirit" (20:23).

The Spirit is given only when Jesus is glorified; that is, he is given as the fruit of the paschal mystery. God's life is in us only because his Son gave himself on the cross for the life of the world, and gave himself to us to live in us through the gift of the Holy Spirit. To receive the body and blood of Jesus in the Eucharist is to receive a new outpouring of the Holy Spirit, provided we are rightly disposed for this gift.

The Holy Spirit, the living source of life, lives in the believer. But even when he lives in us, the Spirit is ever flowing to us from Jesus who has been lifted up and glorified. From now and on into eternity, we will be living God's life only in Jesus, incessantly receiving from him, as from a gushing fountain, the life-giving Spirit. God, "the source of living waters," is incessantly giving his life to us in his Son, who is forever pouring out the Spirit into believers to keep this divine life alive in them.

The nature of God is ever-flowing life. God is the fullness of life flowing among the three divine Persons. This life overflows to us. It is the gift of God given to us by Jesus, God's only begotten Son. "The Word became flesh and made his dwelling among us . . . full of grace and truth. . . . From his fullness we have all received" (1:14-16).

All that we have written so far in this chapter was inspired by a simple comment of St. Thomas Aquinas in his *Commentary on John* (4):

> The living water signifies the grace of the Holy Spirit. The water is living because it is inseparable from its source. The grace of the Holy Spirit is rightly called living water, because the grace of the Holy Spirit is given in such a way that the very source of grace is given, namely, the Holy Spirit.

By "grace of the Holy Spirit," St. Thomas means what later theologians call sanctifying grace, which is our sharing in God's life. But we share in God's life because the very source of that life dwells within us.

Jesus says all this again in other words later. He says, "The Son gives life to whomever he wishes" (5:21). Then he tells why this is possible. "Just as the Father has life in himself, so also he gave to the Son the possession of life in himself" (5:26).

He says it again later in reference to the Holy Eucharist: "Just as the living Father sent me and I have life because of the Father, so the one who feeds on me will have life because of me" (6:57). Thus again it is clear that the Son gives life to us only as the fruit of his giving of himself on the cross. His preferred way of communicating this life to us is the Eucharist. "Unless you eat the flesh of the Son of Man and drink his blood, you do not have life within you . . . . Whoever eats my flesh and drinks my blood remains in me and I in him" (6:53, 56).

Now we know what the gift of God is and we know who it is who asked the woman for a drink. How do we respond to this knowledge?

"If you knew the gift of God and who is saying to you, 'Give me a drink,' you would have asked him and he would have given you living water" (4:30).

Have you asked? Have you greatly thirsted for this living water as you listened to Jesus and this commentary on his words? If not, perhaps you still do not know in the way Jesus wants you to know. Is your knowledge a loving, savoring knowledge which springs into desire and petition? Is it a contemplative knowledge? Through desire and petition we come to possess the living waters of which Jesus spoke.

Our very being is a thirst for the fullness of life. The thirst of our being should impel us to this desire and petition for the living water, but at first we do not know what we desire. Recall the first words Jesus spoke in John's Gospel, "What are you looking for?" (1:38). We do not really know until a supernatural grace enlightens the natural desire of our heart. Implicitly, Jesus was asking the woman at the well, "What are you thirsting for?" He came to educate the God-given hunger and thirst of our deepest being.

The woman thought she was looking for ordinary water. She came to the well with a water jug. Jesus set about educating her to thirst for the living waters of grace. Only Jesus can give that gift which satisfies the deepest need of human life.

Desire is essential for spiritual growth. One is aroused to desire for two reasons. First, the knowledge of the desirable good: "If you knew the gift of God." Secondly, the knowledge of the giver: "and who is speaking to you . . . you would have asked."

Have you asked for that living water?

John's whole Gospel, we said, is a course in the contemplation of Jesus, the giver of the gift of God. As we come to know Jesus in the depth of our love, beholding him as put before our eyes by the evangelist, desire and petition will spring from our hearts.

In seeking who Jesus is, and what he is for us as the gift of God, we come to see God's own desire, his love's desire to give himself to us in the gift of eternal life. Who was the thirsty one at the well? For what was Jesus thirsting when he asked the woman for a drink? For what was he thirsting at another noon hour when he said from the cross, "I thirst"? God was thirsting for us.

"God so loved the world" — he was so thirsty for us, he so desired to give us eternal life — "that he gave his only Son, so that everyone who believes in him might not perish but might have eternal life" (3:16).

When we lovingly contemplate and savor all this revealed in the Son, the Word, our desire reaches out and meets God's desire. The gift of living waters gushes forth from the pierced side of Jesus upon the cross. Look upon him whom you have pierced! And the living waters within us, the Holy Spirit, will say, "Hasten to the Father!" Satisfy your thirst for life!

13

"Behold Your Mother!"

We do not really see what Jesus invites us to come and see unless he, the Revealer, personally manifests himself to the one who comes. "Contemplate" is not merely something that *we* do. In its deepest, fullest reality it is something the Revealer does in us as he shows himself to us in his intensely personal interior "word" of grace.

Jesus is always the Revealer. If we come to see, we will see only through a direct personal revelation from the ever-present Word. Ours is to need the revelation and desire it. His is to give the personal enlightenment. If you knew the gift of God and who it is who desires to speak this interior personal word of revelation in your heart, you would ask him, and he would give it.

No one fully grasps what the Scriptures are saying unless he or she somehow experiences by grace what the Scriptures are talking about. Thus, the People of God have come to understand the words of Jesus concerning Mary's spiritual motherhood by experiencing Mary's maternal presence.

The Second Vatican Council teaches that the Church has always experienced Mary's maternal presence (*Lumen Gentium*, 62). In his encyclical, *The Mother of the Redeemer*, Pope John Paul II presents our knowledge of Mary as the

Church has come to know her from reflecting through the centuries, in the light of the Scriptures, upon this experience of Mary's ever-continuing presence among us. The pope speaks about two modes of Mary's continuing presence in the Church: her active presence and her exemplary presence.

Mary is actively present in the Church as our mother endowed with maternal love and real power to assist us in our pilgrimage of faith. And she is present with us as our exemplar, that is, our model in the pilgrimage of faith. She not only made that pilgrimage before us, but she makes it with us, showing us the way.

Let us consider Mary's active presence with us with true maternal power to care for us. Through this maternal power, she is truly involved in the whole life of the Church. John the Evangelist was the one privileged by God to tell us in his Gospel about our Lady's full involvement in the paschal mystery. This is the mystery of the suffering, death and resurrection of the Lamb of God sacrificed on the cross for the salvation of the world.

John shows us how Mary is involved not only in that phase of the paschal mystery which was accomplished on Calvary where our Paschal Lamb was sacrificed. She is fully involved, too, in every phase of that mystery as it is being accomplished in God's people till the end of time, for the paschal mystery is completed only when it is fulfilled in us.

John tells us all of this in the Cana/Calvary story. For John, the story of the wedding feast of Cana and the story of our Lord's crucifixion on Calvary are one.

This is made clear by John's use of the same key words in both parts of the story. Both at Cana and at Calvary, Jesus addresses Mary as "Woman." On both occasions John says that the mother of Jesus was there. At Cana, Jesus indicates that his "hour" has not yet come; in his prayer at the Last

Supper, he says, "Father, the hour has come! Give glory to your Son, so that your Son may glorify you!" (17:1). He is speaking of his exaltation on the cross where "he revealed his glory" even more fully than he did through the miracle he performed at Cana (2:11). Thus he ties in the events at Cana with those of Calvary.

Cana cannot be understood apart from Calvary, nor can John's presentation of Calvary be understood apart from Cana. John does not tell the Cana story for its own sake. He presents it as a sign pointing to Calvary. The sign at Cana, "the first of his signs" (2:11), helps us interpret the meaning of Calvary where the paschal mystery was accomplished.

Each of the seven signs in John's Gospel points to Calvary. This is made clear in the first of his signs. The sign at Cana points directly to the Lord's "hour," the hour of his glorification on the cross. All the other signs likewise point to that hour. They all help us to understand what took place on Calvary and, specifically, its meaning for us.

In John's sixth chapter, for example, the feeding of five thousand with five loaves is a sign pointing to Calvary where Jesus gives his flesh for the life of the world. Whoever eats his flesh and drinks his blood in the Eucharist has eternal life.

The sign at Cana, "the first of his signs," reveals especially in what way Mary is involved in the paschal mystery of the cross. Her involvement at Cana in maternal concern for human need, such as wine for a wedding, is a symbol of her maternal concern on Calvary for our need of salvation and eternal life.

The sign at Cana interprets the fuller meaning of Mary's presence on Calvary. Cana shows us Mary's heart as she stood at the foot of the cross. It illustrates her maternal role in the work of redemption accomplished on the cross.

Both at Cana and at Calvary Mary is there as mother: "There was a wedding at Cana in Galilee, and the mother of Jesus was there. Jesus and his disciples were also invited to the wedding" (2:1-2). The Son seems to have been invited because of his mother.

The mother is present on Calvary just as she was at Cana. Both at Cana and at Calvary she is involved: "Near the cross of Jesus there stood his mother" (19:25, n). We know from the Cana story that Mary does not just "stand there" at the foot of the cross. Cana, interpreting her presence at "the hour" on Calvary, shows her fully involved with motherly solicitude for all of us. Mary at "the hour" is to be seen with all the characteristics she displayed at Cana.

Because of his mother, Jesus was invited to Cana, and at Cana, because of his mother, Jesus went into action, changing water into wine at her request. She is the Mediatrix whose maternal intercession at Cana, and therefore at Calvary, brings his saving power into action.

Both at Cana and at Calvary it is maternal intercession at work, and so too her continuing active presence in the Church is her presence and power through maternal intercession, as the paschal mystery is formed in each one of us.

The image of Mary interceding at Cana is a revelation that her role in the paschal mystery of Jesus is one of intercession. Already at the Annunciation, the desire of her heart was for the salvation of her people. St. Luke presents her, like Simeon and Anna, as one of the poor of Yahweh, those who were "awaiting the consolation of Israel" (Lk 2:25). That desire of her heart was an intercession, for God "fulfills the desire of those who fear him" (Ps 147:19).

That our salvation was always the desire of Mary's heart is revealed also in her Magnificat, her song of joy that God has responded to the needs of his people Israel: "He has helped Israel his servant, remembering his mercy" (Lk 1:54).

Obviously that desire of her heart continued to the end, and her presence at the foot of the cross was an act of intercession for our salvation. Such intercession continues till all the fruits of the paschal mystery have been given to us. By her consent at the Annunciation, Mary dedicated herself to the Person and the work of her Son, and that dedication to the work of our redemption was not revoked on Calvary. Her very presence at the cross expressed her desire for our salvation, and thus was intercession for us.

Jesus responds to that desire of her heart. From the cross, he entrusts the disciple whom he loved to Mary's maternal care and solicitude: "Woman, behold your son!" (19:26). But the disciple whom Jesus loved stood there as a symbol of every true believer, every true disciple. Thus Jesus entrusted every one of us to his mother. He meant each single one of us when he said to her, "Behold your son!"

In response to Mary's motherly concern at Cana, Jesus changed water into wine. So on Calvary, in response to her maternal presence, he hands over to us the new wine, which is the Holy Spirit.

Throughout John's Gospel, Jesus is presented as the one who gives the Holy Spirit. Only after John has established that Mary stood at the cross as a mother concerned for the needs of all does he record that Jesus said, " 'It is finished.' And bowing his head, he handed over the spirit" (19:30). He gives the Holy Spirit as the fruit of his sacrifice. The Spirit then goes to work to form the paschal mystery in each one of us.

Thus Mary is involved not only in the accomplishment of the first phase of the paschal mystery on Calvary. She is involved in its accomplishment in each one of us. Thus the mother of Jesus is the mother of the whole Church. Her intercession at Cana on behalf of the embarrassed couple who had run out of wine is a sign of her continuing intercession till the paschal mystery is completed in all of us. Her involvement in the paschal mystery as she stands beneath the cross of Jesus signifies her continuing maternal involvement in that mystery till it is perfected in each one of us.

Mary is truly present in the whole mystery of the Church, which is simply the continuation and completion of the paschal mystery in each member of Christ. Just as Mary was involved mind and heart in the events of Cana, so she is forever involved mind and heart with every disciple whom Jesus loves; that is, everyone for whom he died. She is "given as mother to every single individual and to all mankind," says Pope John Paul II (MR, 23).

Thus Catholic teaching on Mary as spiritual mother of us all is well grounded in the Cana/Calvary picture in John's Gospel. On Calvary, Jesus specifically commends all of us, represented by the disciple whom he loved, to her maternal care: "Woman, behold your son!"

Mary's title "Woman" given to her by her Son, Jesus, both at Cana and at Calvary, "goes to the very heart of the mystery of Mary," says Pope John Paul II, "and indicates the unique place which she occupies in the whole economy of salvation" (MR, 24).

Jesus called his mother "Woman" in reference to Genesis 3:15, where the Lord God said to the serpent, "I will put enmity between you and the woman." In calling his mother "Woman," Jesus implies that Mary is the new Eve, "the mother of all the living" (Gn 3:20).

Thus far we have been trying to explain Mary's active maternal presence in the Church till the end of time. What about our contemplative response to that presence?

14

Responding To Mary's Presence

Jesus tells us what response he expects to Mary's presence with us when he says to us from the cross, "Behold your mother!"

Motherhood is a personal relationship and calls for a personal relationship in response. The reality "mother" always implies the reality "child," and "child" always implies "mother." So too Mary's spiritual motherhood is a personal relationship with each one of us, and calls for our personal relationship with her in response. Therefore it was not enough for Jesus to say to Mary, "Behold your son." He also had to say to us, "Behold your mother!"

To the heart of each one of us Jesus personally speaks an interior word of grace, saying, "Behold your mother," thus drawing us individually to respond to Mary as our mother. Frequently in the history of the Church people have experienced this word of grace in a vivid way, although to most of us who believe, the word of grace to accept Mary as mother comes so naturally and so easily along with our faith in Jesus that we are not even aware that it is an intimate interior personal invitation from Jesus.

When from the cross, Jesus says to us, "Behold your mother!" he means, first of all, "Accept my mother as your own!" The story of Cana interpreting the meaning of

Calvary shows us how to accept her at the most basic level. In her maternal concern for us, who are represented by the stewards at the wedding feast, she gives us this advice: "Do whatever he tells you!" (2:5). Only if you obey him will you be open to receive the new wine of the Holy Spirit which he pours out as the fruit of his paschal mystery.

"The servants who had drawn the water knew...." We, who are the faithful disciples of the Lord, know from whence the new wine of the Holy Spirit comes. It flows from the pierced heart of Jesus in the hour of his glorification.

Mary's intercession for the wedding couple at Cana symbolizes her intercession for all of us until the paschal mystery finds its fulfillment in our own lives. It is interesting to note here that Mary not only pleads *for* us with God, she also pleads *with* us. She asks us to do his will. In this sense, Mary is truly an "intercessor." The word "intercede" comes from Latin words meaning "to go between." Mary is a go-between, an intercessor, a mediator or mediatrix.

A mediator brings parties together by asking something of each. In the Cana/Calvary story, Mary not only appeals to her divine Son to give us the new wine which is the Holy Spirit, she also appeals to us to respond to her Son: "Do whatever he tells you!"

Her intercession with us is as important as her intercession with him. Her maternal work is accomplished only if we respond to her appeal to us and if Jesus responds to her appeal to him.

In all of her reported apparitions throughout the centuries, Mary is always seen appealing to us. Her repeated calls to repentance, for example, are calls to turn from the disobedience of sin to the obedience of faith: "Do whatever he tells you!"

Obedience is the essence of the paschal mystery. Jesus was obedient unto death, even death on the cross.

Mary's motherly function in our lives is to bring us to obey her Son, and thus to obey God the Father. This is summed up in her appeal, "Do whatever he tells you!" Her motherly function on our behalf is frustrated by our disobedience to her Son.

It is presumptuous to call on Mary as our mother while resisting her Son at the same time. If we remain in rebellion against her Son, our heavenly mother can do nothing for us. Her maternal work as refuge of sinners is to call forth from sinners the courage and willingness to change their hearts and ways. Only through conversion can we who are sinners benefit from her maternal care.

In all of this, Mary shares in the mission of her Divine Son who is the one Mediator between God and human beings. "He lives forever to make intercession for them," we read in Hebrews 7:25. From the cross he fulfilled this role in an eminent fashion when he prayed, "Father, forgive them for they know not what they do" (Lk 23:34).

But Jesus also appeals incessantly to us to do God's will: "Whoever does the will of God is my brother and sister and mother" (Mk 3:35). "Not everyone who says to me, 'Lord, Lord,' will enter the kingdom of heaven, but only the one who does the will of my Father in heaven" (Mt 7:21). There is no other way to union with God. Jesus alone is the Way, the Truth and the Life.

Look Lovingly and Intently at Mary

There is another level on which we need to respond to Mary's maternal presence in the Church. This, too, is expressed in Jesus' words to us, "Behold your mother!" In John's Gospel, as we have seen, the word "Behold" means "Look closely, fix your attention upon." Therefore when

Jesus says, "Behold your mother," he means, "Look intently upon her. Fix your love and affection upon her. Contemplate her."

This is what Pope John Paul II means when he speaks in his encyclical of Mary's continuing presence in the Church as exemplar and model of our pilgrimage of faith. If we look intently and lovingly at Mary, we will come to see that her whole life is focused totally on Jesus in the obedience which is faith.

In John's Gospel, the word "Behold" usually announces a divine revelation, a divine truth which we must contemplate in faith and love, a truth which, like Mary (Lk 2:19), we must ponder in our hearts in loving and attentive faith.

Contemplating lovingly inevitably gets us involved with what we see and love. As we contemplate our mother, we get involved in a loving relationship with her, and in her loving relationship with her Son.

At Cana, Mary was told equivalently by Jesus, "Come and see!" For when she said, "They have no wine," Jesus at once pointed her attention to "the hour," the hour of his paschal sacrifice on the cross. In pointing to his hour, Jesus is telling his Mother to contemplate him in a new light, to see him in a new way.

When she does this, she comes to behold her Son as the sacrificed Lamb of God, and in love she gets fully involved in his paschal mystery. When Jesus says to her at the foot of the cross, "Woman, behold your son," she learns to behold her Son Jesus in all those who are born from above by the power of the Holy Spirit who flows out to us like water from the pierced side of the Lamb.

Thus as she contemplates the mystery of her Son, she learns to extend her maternal solicitude beyond the earthly needs of the couple at Cana to the spiritual needs of all her spiritual children. She seeks to obtain for them the spiritual realities symbolized by the wine at Cana, the new wine of the Holy Spirit.

When, therefore, Jesus says to us, "Behold your mother," he means first of all, "I reveal her to you as your mother. Accept her as your own!" But he also means, "Lovingly fix your attention upon her. Contemplate her. Come to know what it means that she is your mother. Only thus can you fully respond to my gift of her to you. She is your mother only because of her total involvement in my suffering, death and resurrection. Behold her involvement and get involved with me in my paschal mystery the way she did.

"In short, behold her faith. She is the model of your pilgrimage of faith. I said to her, as I said to John's disciples, 'Come and see!' She came and she saw. She pondered everything in her heart (Lk 2:19, 51). Behold me in the way she did, and you, too, will come to see all that she beheld."

15

The Seven "I AM" Statements

When Jesus uses the words "I AM" with a predicate, he always uses the definite article with the predicate. He does not say, for example, "I am bread," but "I am *the* bread." He doesn't say, "I am a shepherd," but "I am *the* shepherd." He is not merely a particular example of a general class. He identifies himself with the class. He is the class.

A noun used as a predicate usually lacks a specifying article, for ordinarily it simply indicates a general class of which the subject is only one example. All kinds of bread belong to the general class "bread." Rye bread can say, "I am bread." Barley bread and wheat loaves and corn bread can all say the same. But when the definite article is used, it indicates that the predicate is identical with the subject: Joe is the one!

Jesus is the light of the world. And, conversely, the light of the world is Jesus, and no other. The emphasis lies on the identity and interchangeability of subject and predicate. The bread of life is Jesus. Jesus is the bread of life. The truth is Jesus. Jesus is the truth.

In hearing Jesus say, "I am the bread," we do not assume that we know what bread is in the ordinary sense, and then apply this to Jesus metaphorically. Jesus is not merely saying, "I am like bread." On the contrary, Jesus is what "bread" or "shepherd" or "light" or "life" basically means. And it is the ordinary meanings of the words that are metaphorical.

Ordinary bread, and light, and life are like Jesus in some small way. According to the Scriptures, all things were created to manifest God. For example, material bread was so created by God that it would reveal to us something about God and Jesus. In saying, "I am the bread," Jesus is saying, "I am not like bread. Bread is like me." Bread is patterned after me, not I after bread. I am not like shepherds. Shepherds are like me. Shepherds are made in my likeness, not I in theirs. Bread tells you something about what I am for you. Light tells you something about what I am for you. Only God, and Jesus who is one with God, is our life, our light, our nourishment, our guide. Only absolute life, not the relative, can satisfy us:

> Whoever comes to me will never hunger,
> whoever believes in me will never thirst (6:35).

Because Jesus is I AM, God present among us, he is bread, life, light, way, truth, the good shepherd, and so on. Only I AM satisfies all desire, every need, every longing. Nothing else is adequate.

Thus Jesus is the revelation that God is our all, and Jesus is the gift of that all to us. All is given to us in him: bread, life, light, truth, guidance, resurrection.

On the seven occasions that Jesus uses I AM with a predicate, he says seven things about himself:

1. I am the bread of life (6:35, 41, 48, 51).
2. I am the light of the world (8:12; 9:5).
3. I am the gate (10:7, 9).
4. I am the good shepherd (10:11, 14).

5. I am the resurrection and the life (11:25).
6. I am the way and the truth and the life (14:6).
7. I am the true vine (15:1, 5).

The predicate in all seven "I AM" statements tells us what God is for us. But what God is for us, he is through Jesus and in Jesus. Jesus is what he is for us only because of what he is in himself. He is the I AM which is God present to us. "Just as the living Father sent me and I have life because of the Father, so also whoever feeds on me will have life because of me" (6:57).

The "I AM" statements are all revelations of God's self-giving. God so loved the world that he gave his only Son. But the gift of his Son is the gift of himself. Yahweh speaks his sevenfold "I AM" to us in Jesus, and he gives this "I AM" (that is, all that he is for us) in Jesus. The seven "I AM" statements reveal the thoroughness of God's self-giving.

Thus the "I AM" statements are a revelation not only of what God is for us, but are the revelation of the actual gift of all this in Jesus. Light and life, bread of life, resurrection and life, way, truth and life, resurrection from sin, are all given in the sacrificed I AM on the cross:

> If you do not believe that I AM
> you shall die in your sins (8:24).

Only I AM, lifted up on the cross as the Lamb of God, takes away the sins of the world. Jesus might well have said also, "I am the forgiveness of sins."

Thus all the I AM statements are like a commentary on that key verse, "God so loved the world that he gave his only Son" (3:16). For God's will to be our bread, our light, our way, our truth, our life is sealed in his gift of his Son. Everything is already given to us in the Son. "For God so loved the world that he gave his only Son." We have only to accept the gift.

All of this is what we come to see when we accept the invitation of Jesus, "Come and you will see."

16

"Whom Are You Looking For?"

In the garden, on the morning of his resurrection, Jesus said to Mary Magdalene, "Whom are you looking for?" (20:15).

The One whom Mary Magdalene seeks and finds in the garden of burial is the one who called himself, "I AM." At first she sees him as the gardener (20:15). Then she sees him as her beloved rabbi, her teacher who had drawn her heart by the power of his word (20:16). But now he reveals himself for who he really is by describing the fullness of salvation he has brought by his presence among us as *EGO EIMI*, the only saving God: "I am ascending to my Father and your Father, my God and your God" (20:17). Here we have come full circle from the Prologue's statement, "To those who received him by believing in his name, he gave power to become children of God" (1:12). His Father is now their Father, his God is their God. As children of God, they have eternal life even now. And with Jesus they are ascending to the Father, for they have been "born from above."

Mary Magdalene must no longer see him as only a rabbi at whose feet she can sit, not even the Rabbi par excellence. "Stop holding on to me," he tells her (20:17). Stop holding on to your old way of seeing me. See me henceforth as one glorified with the Father with the glory I had with him before the world began. The Son of Man who descended from heaven has ascended to where he was before.

What has Mary Magdalene seen? "I have seen the Lord!" she exclaims to the disciples (20:18). She has seen the One whom a week later the believing Thomas will address as "My Lord and my God!" (20:28).

"My Lord and my God!" We call him that because we see in him all that we discover when we fix our eyes and hearts attentively upon him in answer to the Baptist's indication, "Behold the Lamb of God," and Jesus' invitation, "Come and you will see." In seeing him as Lord and God we see everything he has revealed about himself as Lamb of God — who he is in himself, and what he is for us.

Behold the Lamb of God! Behold him daily in the Eucharist! Behold him always and everywhere present in power to save!

Whom Are You Looking For?

The full divinity of Jesus is implied when he says to those who come out to arrest him, "*EGO EIMI*, I AM" (18:5, 6). " 'Whom are you looking for?' he asked them. They answered, 'Jesus, the Nazorean.' He said to them, '*EGO EIMI* (I AM)' " (18:5). "When he said to them, 'I AM,' they turned away and fell to the ground" (18:6). They are stunned, as it were, by the divine presence and power. The serene divine majesty of Jesus is contrasted with the confusion of the arresting party.

In the garden when he is arrested, Jesus asks, "Whom are you looking for?" (18:4), and in the garden where he had been buried, he asks Mary Magdalene, "Whom are you looking for?" (20:15). Thus we come full circle to the first question Jesus spoke in John's Gospel when he said to the first two disciples who began to follow him, "What are you looking for?" (1:38). It is not a something we are looking for. We are looking for a living Person, and his name is "I AM."

Whether we know it or not, I AM is the one we all seek. We seek our saving God, as our light and our life. We find him present among us in Jesus who says to us all, "I AM, the one who is speaking to you" (4:29). To reject our God present in Jesus is to die in our sins. To accept him is to have eternal life.

These last two times that Jesus asks, "Whom are you looking for?" (18:5 and 20:15), highlight both the tragedy and the glory dramatized throughout John's Gospel. Some fail miserably in life's quest and die in their sins because they refuse to believe in the name of the only Son of God. Others find all that they were seeking. By believing in his name, they find life in him who is Life itself.

Both the tragedy and the glory are expressed in John's Prologue. The tragedy: "He came to what was his own, but his own people did not accept him" (1:11). The glory: "But to those who did accept him, who believed in his name, he gave power to become children of God" (1:12).

An Interesting Thought

The publication you have just finished reading is part of the apostolic efforts of the Society of St. Paul of the American Province. The Society of St. Paul is an international religious community located in 23 countries, whose particular call and ministry is to bring the message of Christ to all people through the communications media.

Following in the footsteps of their patron, St. Paul the Apostle, priests and brothers blend a life of prayer and technology as writers, editors, marketing directors, graphic designers, bookstore managers, pressmen, sound engineers, etc. in the various fields of the mass media, to announce the message of Jesus.

If you know a young man who might be interested in a religious vocation as a brother or priest and who shows talent and skill in the communications arts, ask him to consider our life and ministry. For more information at no cost or obligation write:

Vocation Office
2187 Victory Blvd.
Staten Island, NY 10314-6603
Telephone: (718) 698-3698